THE TRUTH IS

1. Leveling up your craft to write a story that lives long after you've left the planet is what some might call a ridiculous goal.

2. You know that you will not tell that story after reading just one how-to-write book.

3. You know that you will not tell that story as the result of taking one seminar.

4. You know that creating a timeless work of art will require the dedication of a world-class athlete. You will be training your mind with as much ferocity and single-minded purpose as an Olympic gold medal hopeful. That kind of cognitive regimen excites you, but you just haven't found a convincing storytelling dojo to do that work.

5. The path to leveling up your creative craft is a dark and treacherous course. You've been at it a long time, and it often feels like you're wearing three-dimensional horse blinders. More times than you'd wish to admit, you're not sure if you are moving north or south or east or west. And the worst part? You can't see anyone else, anywhere going through what you're going through. You're all alone.

WELCOME TO THE STORY GRID UNIVERSE. HERE'S HOW WE CONTEND WITH THOSE TRUTHS:

1. We believe we find meaning in the pursuit of creations that last longer than we do. It is *not* ridiculous. Dedicating our work to seizing opportunities and overcoming obstacles as we stretch ourselves to reach for seemingly unreachable creations is transformational. We believe this pursuit is the most valuable and honorable way to spend our time here. Even if...especially if...we never reach our lofty creative goals.

2. Writing just one story isn't going to take us to the top. We're moving from point A to Point A^{5000}. We've got lots of mountains to climb, lots of rivers and oceans to cross, and many deep dark forests to traverse in our way. We need topographic guides on demand, and if they're not available now, we'll have to figure it out and write them ourselves.

3. While we're drawn to seminars to consume the imparted wisdom from an icon in the arena, we leave with something far more valuable than the curriculum. We get to meet the universe's other pilgrims and compare notes on the terrain.

4. The Story Grid Universe has a virtual dojo, a university to work out and get stronger—the place to stumble, correct the mistakes, and stumble again until the moves become automatic, lethal, and mesmerizing to outside observers.

5. The Story Grid Universe has a performance space, a publishing house dedicated to leveling up the craft with clear boundaries of progress, and the ancillary reference resources to pack for each project mission. There is an infinite number of paths to where you want to be with a story that works.

Seeing how others made it down their own private yellow brick roads to release their creations into the timeless creative cosmos will help keep you on the straight and narrow path.

All are welcome—the more, the merrier—but please abide by the golden rule.

Put the Work Above All Else, and trust the process.

THE WONDERFUL WIZARD OF OZ BY L. FRANK BAUM

A STORY GRID MASTERWORKS ANALYSIS GUIDE

SHAWN COYNE

Edited by
LESLIE WATTS

STORY GRID

STORY GRID

Story Grid Publishing LLC
223 Egremont Plain Road
PMB 191
Egremont, MA 01230

First Story Grid Publishing Paperback Edition December 2020

For Information About Special Discounts for Bulk Purchases,

Please visit www.storygridpublishing.com

ISBN: 978-1-64501-056-2
Ebook: 978-1-64501-041-8

For

All Past, Present, and Future Story Nerds

HOW TO READ THE WONDERFUL WIZARD OF OZ BY L. FRANK BAUM: A STORY GRID MASTERWORKS ANALYSIS GUIDE

There are two ways to read this book.

1. Enjoy the novel without worrying about any of the Story Grid stuff.

2. Read each chapter thinking about the Story Grid principles.

    a) The bolded words in each scene correspond to a particular element that Story Gridders would include on their Story Grid Spreadsheet. To see the entire Story Grid Spreadsheet for *The Wonderful Wizard of Oz* (it's far too long and detailed to include in this book), visit https://www.storygrid.com/masterwork/The-Wonderful-Wizard-of-Oz/.

    Please note some bolded sections within the text are not part of the Story Grid Spreadsheet. I've highlighted them to point out a particular telling passage from the book.

    b) Occasionally, you'll see an italicized notation within the text. They are there to indicate a particular creative choice the writer made or to pinpoint a particular storytelling technique, like point of view or the controlling idea.

c) At the conclusion of each scene, I've included an additional section entitled *Analyzing the Scene*. By answering four Socratic questions, I'll walk you through how to determine the critical information for the Story Grid Spreadsheet—*Story Event* and *Value Shift*.

d) Another section I've included at the end of each scene is "How the Scene Abides by the Five Commandments of Storytelling."

For each and every scene in *The Wonderful Wizard of Oz*, I indicate the Inciting Incident, Turning Point Progressive Complication, Crisis, Climax, and Resolution.

For those unfamiliar with Story Grid's Five Commandments of Storytelling, you can read about them in the book *Story Grid 101* (free download on the Story Grid site), in *The Story Grid*: *What Good Editors Know*, or in articles about them on the site. Just access the "start here" or "resources" section of https://www.s-torygrid.com/ to read at your leisure.

e) In addition to the Story Grid Spreadsheet for *The Wonderful Wizard of Oz*, you can view the Story Grid Foolscap and the actual Story Grid Infographic at https://www.storygrid.-com/masterwork/The-Wonderful-Wizard- of-Oz/.

A WHOLE GREATER THAN THE SUM OF ITS PARTS

If you want to write stories that sell, one of the best things you can do is study stories like *The Wonderful Wizard of Oz* by L. Frank Baum, which continues to sell and delight readers more than one hundred years after it was published. It's what we in the Story Grid Universe call a masterwork.

What do we mean by that?

Masterworks are stories readers come back to again and again because *they get it right*. They're at the top of their particular genre, but more important, masterworks stick with us because their whole is far more potent than the sum of their three macro storytelling parts.

What are those three parts? A primal Action Story, a transformational Worldview Story, and a transcendent Heroic Journey 2.0 story.

What about these parts attracts readers to a wide variety of stories? Each component generates emotion in the audience by setting up and ultimately paying off a fundamental question.

1. With its on-the-surface life-and-death stakes for all four of its central characters (Dorothy, Scarecrow, Tin Woodman, and Lion), *The Wonderful Wizard of Oz* is a primal Action Story.

This primal action component generates audience excitement by posing and answering a fundamental question. Will they survive the unexpected challenges arising from the external and internally mediated social environments?

2. With its above-the-surface expansion in cognitive-capacity for all four of its central characters, *The Wonderful Wizard of Oz* is a transformational worldview story.

This transformational worldview component generates audience empathy by posing and answering a second fundamental question. How will they generate the cognitive power to thrive and attain their individual and collective goals while navigating an unpredictable, life-threatening environment?

3. With its beyond-the-surface expression of the will to go on despite uncertain success and certain mortality, *The Wonderful Wizard of Oz* is a transcendent Heroic Journey 2.0 story.

The Heroic Journey 2.0 component generates audience catharsis by posing and answering the final fundamental question. Will they discover the complex truth about themselves as agents embedded inside a paradoxical universe both ordered and chaotic?

If, as I propose, *The Wonderful Wizard of Oz* is a timeless masterwork that enthralls generation after generation of readers because of the compelling execution of these three macro story forms simultaneously, which inherently pose and then answer three intriguing questions ...

Where did these questions come from?

PERENNIAL PROBLEMS

From the cradle to the grave, no matter if we are citizens of the Lakota Nation or Scarsdale residents or live in vans down by the river, we all have three big abstract existential problems.

Suppose we were able to put history's broadest cultural spectrum of philosophers in one big conference room with an unlimited supply of coffee and donuts to identify the primary challenges we face as humans. In that case, these three perennial problems would emerge at the top of their list of what abstractly ails our species. *Homo sapiens* conundrums boil down into three fundamental categories.

Broadly put, these problems are what every single member of *Homo sapiens* faces "today." Our descendants will face these problems tomorrow too. Not surprisingly, they are derived from what every single member of *Homo sapiens* met in the past.

What would the worldly philosophers conclude?

Let's personalize them.

How do I survive?
How do I thrive?
How do I derive existential meaning?

That's it. Isn't it? Because every other problem we encounter fits within one of these categories.

We first have to meet our physiological needs (survive) to concentrate on generating the power to secure our continued well-being (thrive) to ultimately figure out who we are, why we're here, and what we ought to do about those truths (derive).

The individual must 1) stay alive, and then 2) summon the power to pursue goals beyond survival and 3) figure out the truth of who they are, why they're here, and how to behave to realize their particular purpose.

The grand thesis of Story Grid's Heroic Journey 2.0 (HJ2.0) is that our ancestors gave us far more useful earthly navigational direction than "grow up" or "follow your bliss." HJ2.0 is a synthesis of Carl Jung's seventy-plus-year-old monomythic fueled Individuation Process (which was mechanized by Joseph Campbell and Christopher Vogler as "The Hero's Journey") through the prism of contemporary cognitive science.

I propose that what's embedded inside stories from the past like *The Wonderful Wizard of Oz* is a sort of operator's manual for human life containing the semantic information we need to solve our perennial lurking problems from the past in our present. This process enables us to meaningfully grow as individuals and, by extension, affords us the collective capacity to survive as a species into the future.

Action Story concerns the primary representations of objectively measurable physical bodies' movements, including the overt utterances of *Homo sapiens* speech or what characters do and say. This arc involves the literal, observable, technical, and specific physical behaviors of a being through time and space. It's the realm of the objective.

Worldview Story concerns the secondary representations (individual qualia) of subjective applications of the mind or the way characters think about themselves and their world. This arc involves transforming the beings' integrated strategy (worldview) and specific behavioral tactics (personas enacted overtly or covertly) to optimize their power. The technique and tactics enable the beings to pay attention to and process the combinatorially explosive amounts of information that floods their senses in any given context.

Worldview is about how the mind transforms the way it processes the multitude of sensory information from the external and socio-cultural environment and changes its behavior as a result. It's the realm of the subjective.

HJ2.0 concerns attuning the "transjective" relationship between ourselves and our universal arena. The universal arena includes not only the external world and all the people and objects within it but also the complex social systems from our closest *first-party* family affiliations, to our *second-party* tribal affiliations (limited by our human Dunbar number), to our *third-party* mass population affiliations, and ultimately to the collective cognitive capacities of our entire species through time.

Transjective refers to properties, not of the subject or the object environment, but the relationships between them. So, there's the object (the objective), the observer of the object (the subjective), and the relationship between the two and the universal arena (the transjective).

HJ2.0 is a mythic representation of how we come into our "personhood," owning a fluid psyche capable of generating wise agency in and through time by clearly attuning the objective, subjective, and transjective in the short, medium, and long term.

In other words, Action Story concerns our efforts to survive—Schopenhauer's "will to live." Worldview Story concerns our efforts to thrive—Nietzsche's "will to power." And HJ2.0 concerns our efforts to derive wisdom—Kierkegaard and Frankl's "will to meaning."

Timeless, inexhaustibly meaningful masterworks are the equivalent of what we at Story Grid conceptualize as a high signal ancestral internet, artificial intelligence 1.0 gifted to us from our wisest predecessors.

These masterworks serve us as sticky and spreadable interpersonal communication devices that advise us how to behave to generate our greatest chance to cultivate collective human wisdom through time. Conforming to these patterns not only ensures the continuation of our species but confers an adaptive advantage to the individual creator.

In other words, because they ring true to us and pack an emotional punch, stories that embed HJ2.0 sell at a more consistent and escalating rate through time than those that don't.

Story Grid is a methodology to crack open the seal of masterworks to reveal the messages in the bottles our ancestors dropped into the swirling ocean of time to guide our best navigational course as individuals. And as a byproduct, it can transform a story that doesn't work commercially into one that does.

Before we get into the granular scene-by-scene analysis of *The Wonderful Wizard of* Oz, let's look at the nature and function of story and use Story Grid's five macro stages of the Heroic Journey 2.0 to lay out the global movement of L. Frank Baum's masterwork as a pitch-perfect example of the ancestral internet's singular signal.

THE BIG IDEA OF THE HEROIC JOURNEY 2.0

Story Grid's HJ2.0 is all about clarifying what we as a species use story for. What are its nature and function?

Here's what I've been going on about for decades.

I maintain that stories are simulations, or "counterfactual scenarios," that allow us to observe from a safe distance the fallout from unexpected events. All that means is they are "make 'em ups" about what might happen when a force of change drops into a *Homo sapiens*-modeled life.

From the creator's point of view (the storyteller), if "x" were to happen, there is a reasonable probability "y" would spool out as a result. *X* equals the force of change in a Global Inciting Incident that threatens or advances a protagonist's (or group of protagonists') ability to survive, thrive, and derive existential meaning. *Y* is the resulting change in the protagonist and the universal arena.

What is the nature of that unexpected event? Psychologically, these external forces of change reflect the repeating pattern of the protagonist's yet-to-be-solved abstract unconscious problems. The protagonist must confront and metabolize the change event, which forces them to break and remake their worldview. The result is either a reciprocal opening and attunement of the protagonist to their experiential arena or a joint narrowing of the protagonist and their experiential arena. They expand their world, or they contract their world.

We use stories to prime the pumps of our imagination when we face changes in our environments. They serve as positive prescriptions and negative cautions to consider while plotting our path through time inside our particular ontological and epistemological frameworks (our idiosyncratic worldviews).

All of that is to say we see our lives as internal stories and thus map our life events onto stories we expose ourselves to.

What's been bothering me is that these prescriptions and cautions are all well and good, but unless we understand the ultimate destination or message, aren't they simply propaganda arguments to get us to see the world as the story creator sees it?

The answer is yes. The storyteller's controlling idea is, for lack of a better description, "what they are selling" to their potential audience.

The audience is searching for meaningful intelligence to inform their worldview so they can attune to a higher level of reality. We want to better understand the arena we must navigate including the external environment, our relationships with other humans, and our internal landscape. Thus story-engagers expend substantial amounts of cognitive energy to enter the world of a story.

But to what end?

Being informed by a story to help us attain goal states is useful, but soon a question arises. Is there a meta-goal state? A single operating principle that confers adaptive advantage for the individual and extends all the way up to the species?

I propose there is. In my years analyzing contemporary and perennial masterworks, I've found an extraordinary reoccurring phenomenon. The stories that last, the ones written generations ago that we still read today, share a whole slew of features in common. Abstractly, these stories offer a meta-goal for the individual and, taken to the end of the line, the species.

What's remarkable is that there is no single goal state, no Nirvana or utopic destination offered in these timeless masterworks. Instead, a process is on offer. The reason is that the universe is a paradox, made up of a complex mix of order and chaos. We cannot predict with certainty what will happen next. And because change is the only constant we can rely on, there is no ideal result where everything remains stable and perfect. Disruption is the generator function of the system. So, we must adapt and roll with the changes.

What's on offer in the HJ2.0 is simply a navigational process that increases the probability of surviving, thriving, and deriving meaning. The individual gets to choose whether they follow its demanding and painful course. If most of us do, we increase the probability for all of us to continue to exist. If most of us don't, we decrease the probability for all of us to continue to exist. This is the purest signal of the HJ2.0.

The growth process embedded within these stories informs us about the most sensible navigational path, one we can use to guide our physical, meta-physical, and spiritual growth.

My findings are not unique.

Instead, they support the central idea Carl Jung introduced in 1935. His individuation process is the abstract structural and functional organization of stories that spread and last.

Jung proposes that our species has a North Star monomythic structure, a process by which the individual can survive, thrive, and derive meaning beyond the primary, objective, science-based representations of our physical existence. All that means is that Jung maintained that we are more than our atoms, molecules, and cellular systems that some popularly refer to as a "meat sack."

How did he reach this conclusion? He read a lot of stories across multiple traditions and compared and contrasted them. He documented our species' rich storytelling tradition and the recurring patterns of representational behavior embedded inside stories across cultures and time.

Jung dedicated himself to exploring the secondary representations of our metaphysical existence—in other words, the subjective qualities of reality rather than just the measurable objective scientific quantities. He focused on the stories' thematic attributes rather than the characters' literal descriptions and actions. By doing so, he was able to uncover the best practices to attune the "transjective" relationships between our objective and subjective experiences.

He put forward that the most well-known and oldest stories are about how an individual member of *Homo sapiens* must undertake a mission into unfamiliar terrain to level up into a higher realm of consciousness and become better attuned to the paradoxical circumstances of our existence.

Let's be more specific about what he was getting at and walk through Jung's idea using Story Grid's language.

THE HJ2.0 GLOBAL INCITING INCIDENT

At the beginning of a story, something happens to the protagonist that they cannot "see," let alone understand. It will require the entire length and breadth of the story to realize what "that happening" means to them personally and to the species collectively.

It's important to emphasize that the protagonist doesn't even "see" the vector/force, which will require them to change, for what it truly represents.

That vector/force is the Global Inciting Incident, the drop-in of an unexpected phenomenon, and what I call an "Invisible Phere Gorilla," a concept derived from the invisible gorilla experiment by Christopher Chabris and Daniel Simons. The experiment revealed that people can become blind to unexpected events happening in front of them when focused on a goal.[1]

These Global Inciting Incidents are so complex and deeply rooted in the protagonist's unconscious that they are utterly oblivious to their reoccurrence. Think of the film *Groundhog Day* or the Netflix series *Russian Doll*, which brings back the same change-inducing phenomenon over and over again. Until the protagonist solves this reoccurring Invisible Phere Gorilla problem, they will suffer the consequences of the same problem resurfacing in their life. They must dare to apply their energy and attention to figure out what it exactly means to them.

These invisible Phere Gorillas have paradoxical philosophical origins. Through the lens of science, they would be classified as random instances of change that drop into the protagonist's life from the universal arena with no rhyme or reason. They are objectively definable ... like the Cyclone in *The Wonderful Wizard of Oz*.

But through the lens of the humanities, invisible Phere Gorillas represent recurring patterns that bubble up from the protagonist's or the collective unconscious. They are subjectively definable as triggers for maladaptive behaviors that the protagonist must correct or level up before they can reach a higher state of consciousness. They represent patterns of behavior adopted in the past to survive unmetabolized trauma in the short term. But now they have proven to be long-term behavioral liabilities.

The storyteller is required to understand and consider both the objective and subjective components of the change vector/inciting incident. What is the objective, measurable, concretely definable component, and what is the subjective meaning of the stimulus to the protagonist?

For example, relieving stress by having an evening cocktail is a short-term solution for "having a tough day." But if that behavior turns into a habitual response to stress, it can prove to be a tough habit to break. An aid can quickly become both a physiological and psychological necessity. And soon "not having a cocktail" is unimaginable. To a carpenter, every problem looks like a "hammer-solution." And to an alcoholic, every problem looks like a "cocktail-solution."

Dissociating from one's body if one has been physically or mentally abused is another deeply rooted short-term self-preservation strategy. If someone suffers prolonged abuse, the dissociation behavior becomes a habitual "go-to" for an ever-increasing category of negative objective and subjective experiences.

So, if the people responsible for protecting the protagonist turned out to be abusive, unsympathetic and unempathetic to their being ... then the first principle the protagonist will develop to protect themselves is that all human beings are abusive, uncaring and unempathetic to their being.

When the protagonist experiences similar environmental conditions and receives identical emotional messages from their limbic system that they've had in the past, the character goes into DEFCON 1 habitual behavior programming. They'll automatically output "dissociation" or another short-term adaptive but long-term maladaptive behavior.

The entire story concerns the protagonist's need to confront the awful truth that they have employed a worldview that includes dependence upon one of these faulty first principles as its foundation.

As individuals we *Homo sapiens* are not aware of when our internal protective behavioral programs that were effective short term transform into liabilities long term.

The truth is so harrowing for the individual with traumatic experience (these behaviors had been the last best hope for survival) that they strenuously avoid going near them intellectually to stand them down.

That makes biological sense because of the pleasure/pain principle. Our internal short-term thinker has no use for pain. They just want to stay alive, keep calm, and carry on with minimal discomfort.

So HJ2.0 is all about the protagonist going through the extraordinarily painful process of discovering "what ails them." Learning what short-term adaptive code proves to be long-term maladaptive code is the first stage to correct their cognitive processes to sustain their life, power, and meaning-making growth.

The real rub here is that this code forms the foundation of the protagonist's entire worldview. To break that code apart requires a complete fracturing of the system that has taken care of them since they can't remember when. To undergo such dissolution is the most painful psychological torment imaginable.

Thus, it requires extraordinary courage and the acceptance of monumental loss.

But, to do so proves miraculous. For just as the final worldview principle breaks, a new, more accurately attuned worldview emerges. A revelatory insight comes to the protagonist—one that proves to be more meaningful than any other they've ever considered. From this bedrock of understanding, a more adaptive, better-attuned worldview emerges.

Jung called the process of breaking and remaking one's worldview framing individuation. Contemporary cognitive scientists have another phrase for breaking and remaking frame—insight.

So, the Global Inciting Incident of a HJ2.0 Story must be about a recurring abstract change-inducing stimulus that drops into a protagonist's life and outputs a complicated, autonomic habitual series of long-term maladaptive behaviors.

At the beginning of the story, the protagonist is clueless about the Invisible Phere Gorilla or what it means. They don't even see it.

This kick-off event for HJ2.0 raises two subliminal questions in the minds of the audience. Will the protagonist(s) discover the truth about their maladaptive worldview? And as agents with agency, will they afford their emergent development after confronting this truth?

THE HJ2.0 GLOBAL INCITING INCIDENT OF THE WONDERFUL WIZARD OF OZ

Let's get specific.

I'm proposing that *The Wonderful Wizard of Oz* is a pitch-perfect example of a masterwork. And I'm also offering that masterworks are stories with Jung's individuation process empirically supported by contemporary Cognitive Science, what I'm calling HJ2.0, embedded within them.

So, to support my proposition, I should be able to map the specifics of *The Wonderful Wizard of Oz* onto my abstract notions of what HJ2.0 is.

Let's do that for the Global Inciting Incident for *The Wonderful Wizard of Oz*.

The Global Inciting Incident for the story is the emergence of an extraordinary external environmental change agent, a Kansas Cyclone. It serves as the external force that transports Dorothy into an extraordinary world, but it's an Invisible Phere Gorilla for her because she can't see what it means. She recognizes it as a threat to her survival but nothing more.

Before we move on, let's examine what a cyclone represents meteorologically. What are its objective, scientifically measurable, and categorized components?

A cyclone is a convective storm that generates a gradient of heat transfer. All that means is that hot air rises to the top while the colder air remains at the bottom. The entropic forces that separate the hot and cold create a vortex of air pressure that begins to churn with ever-increasing speed.

What distinguishes a cyclone from a tornado is its size. Tornados produce only one funnel vortex up to hundreds of meters in diameter. Cyclones are much larger, up to hundreds of kilometers in diameter, and can have dozens of vortexes within them.

I don't think it's a coincidence that L. Frank Baum chose a cyclone as his Invisible Phere Gorilla. *The Wonderful Wizard of Oz* is a Worldview Maturation story. It concerns the cognitive development of a bright young girl named Dorothy and the painful process of coming into one's agency, accepting the fallibility of our fellow beings with equanimity, and realizing we're responsible for pursuing the goals we want to achieve. To rely upon magical figures to grant us our desires without our participation is childish.

As we all know, what makes maturation so difficult is the multitude of domain-specific challenges a child faces. These include the forces of socio-cultural systems that emerge from our first, second, and third-party relationships—those we're consciously aware of and those we're not.

They have to contend with metaphysical demands of family, tribal affiliations, and the stringent collective cultural grammar of their historical period. They face the terror of figuring out how to scratch out a means to survive, thrive, and derive an external life entirely on their own in the not too distant future. A multitude of psychic vortexes are at play when we begin the maturation process.

So, as a metaphor, Baum's cyclone was the pitch-perfect choice to externalize the internal maturation problem, a movement from a trinity of undeveloped mind capacities (Jung's self, shadow, and ego) into a coherent, integrated whole. And because he chose to write a story that children would immediately engage with, a constraint he delineates in his introduction, he consolidated his beginning hook into a single chapter. Children's stories are generally constrained by the necessity of having a strong, easy-to-grasp inciting incident in their first scenes.

Baum consciously externalized the painful internal vortex we undergo when we first identify the three components of our psyche, 1) our center of reasoning and higher-order, above-the-surface, abstract thinking (represented by the Scarecrow); 2) our center of on-the-surface power mediated by emotion (represented by the Tin Woodman); and 3) our center of beyond-the-surface interconnectedness with groups enabled by our ability to enact courage (represented by the Lion). Once the child recognizes those three capacities within them, they must integrate the three capacities together so they can coherently apply their unique gifts to solve context-specific problems.

But I'm getting ahead of myself. Let's move on to the next must-have commandment of Storytelling.

THE HJ2.0 GLOBAL TURNING POINT PROGRESSIVE COMPLICATION

Other story theorists often call the Global Turning Point Progressive Complication the "midpoint climax." For Story Grid's HJ2.O, this is the moment when the protagonist's habitual worldview, what I call their worldview 1.0, breaks. And the result of that breakage is that the story's global value at stake shifts to the extraordinarily negative.

Why?

Remember the audience follows the story through the protagonist's point of view or that of a group of protagonists. So, when the protagonist experiences negative stimuli, so does the audience. What happens at this turning point is that what once made sense to the protagonist, no longer does.

Is there anything more damaging than discovering that everything you've come to believe and rely upon to cause the effects that answer your trinity of perennial problems (how to survive, thrive, and derive) no longer work?

That is precisely what's going on in this vital moment in the global story. The protagonist discovers the way they've made it through the world, how they've been causing their desired effects, doesn't work anymore. Nothing makes sense. What they've used to navigate the world is a broken compass leading nowhere. We hit these moments in our lives now and then, and they are terrifying.

Let's back up and link this moment in the story to our Global Inciting Incident, our massive Invisible Phere Gorilla, that will require an entire story to come to grips with.

Thematically the invisible Phere Gorilla is like a child progressively heightening their provocative behavior to seize the full attention of a parent. At this turning point stage, they take their frustration to the end of the line.

Having been ignored for far too long, the Invisible Phere Gorilla manifests its power by breaking the protagonist's worldview frame. Another metaphor I like to use to clarify this moment for myself is to consider that the protagonist is framing the world through a set of eyeglasses. The glasses enable the protagonist to see and make sense of the phenomena surrounding them. Still, these worldview 1.0 lenses do not allow the protagonist to see the critical gorilla causing havoc in their life.

The Global Turning Point Progressive Complication is the moment when the gorilla has had enough. The gorilla grabs the glasses the protagonist is wearing and smashes them to pieces. Now the protagonist can no longer "see." The world they used to navigate relatively easily is now a murky mess—just a big blur.

Losing the ability to coherently categorize and make sense of the environment you find yourself embedded inside is terrifying. Thus, this is a significant moment in the global story. It must be clearly defined in the mind of the storyteller and executed with precision.

Why? If done well, the audience will find themselves as stunned and anxious as the protagonist, which will intrigue them to no end. They feel compelled to keep experiencing the story so they can find satisfaction in its resolution. The audience has experienced this worldview fracture themselves, so they know implicitly if not explicitly what the protagonist is going through. The audience's great relief is that what's happening to the protagonist isn't happening to them. They get to feel the emotions without any of the real-world consequences.

At the highest level of analytical abstraction, the protagonist's experience at the Global Turning Point Progressive Complication is akin to the tremendous opening of cognition observed by people who've used psychedelics to alter their consciousness. These experiences reflect an indescribable (but recognizable) encounter with what the philosopher Immanuel Kant called the numinous. The numinous is the sum total of everything in the universe that we will never be able to know—the Unknown Unknowns.

The prescribed approach to such encounters is to surrender to the experience and allow oneself to be inside the destabilizing random chaotic nothingness without acting. Simply pay attention rather than represent, categorize, symbolize and respond.

Discovering that our worldview isn't working, while terrifying and horrifying, is also enlightening. Problem-solving cannot begin until we've correctly formulated the problem itself. For an amateur carpenter, all problems seem to be hammer problems until they discover other tools.

The Turning Point Progressive Complication is the first stage for the protagonist to return to first-principle thinking to properly formulate the problem represented by the Invisible Phere Gorilla.

More abstractly, at the highest level of HJ2.0, it's the moment when the protagonist directly experiences the inescapable truth of their maladaptive worldview.

THE HJ2.0 GLOBAL TURNING POINT PROGRESSIVE COMPLICATION OF THE WONDERFUL WIZARD OF OZ

At what moment in *The Wonderful Wizard of Oz* is Dorothy's worldview shattered? I propose this moment arises in chapter 15, entitled "The Discovery of Oz the Terrible." Remember that Dorothy, Scarecrow, Tin Woodman, and the Lion initially agreed to Oz's demands that they kill the Wicked Witch of the West and provide proof before he would deign to grant their requests.

In chapter 15, the group returns to the Emerald City to claim their just rewards only to discover ...

Oz is not a wizard. He is incapable of granting the group's wishes.

Dorothy and her friends' worldview—that Oz is a powerful and capable figure who could make their dreams come true as long as they obeyed his authority and did his bidding—crumbles. Oz cannot provide that service. Because he does not possess supernatural capacities, he never could.

As I maintain, *The Wonderful Wizard of Oz* is a Worldview Maturation story. Can you see why this moment aligns with that proposition?

Let's look at this fracturing of worldview through the lens of a *Homo sapiens'* maturation process. When we are born, we are helpless, far more helpless for far longer than any other species on the planet. Because we are vulnerable, our parents must assume the role of solving our perennial problems. They have to ensure that we survive, thrive, and learn how to derive. Adults model the behaviors that provide children meaning. Kids tell their parents' stories to themselves to go about solving problems.

Parents take care of their children's needs and do their best to teach them how to control their desirous wants, play well with others, and make value judgments about "what ought to be."

But there comes a time when the child prepares to take on these burdens for themselves. They start to push outside their home-based comforts to explore the greater world.

And what do they discover? They discover that other *Homo sapiens* out there do not share their parents' strategies and tactics to solve the perennial problems of existence. They find out that others seem to have more or less resources than they do and that the answers their parents have given them prove fallible. There is more than one way to solve a particular problem. Those other individuals may have solved problems more effectively than our parents have.

And ultimately, we discover that merely doing what our parents tell us will not bring us everything we wish to attain. That the prescriptions for success our parents gave us to gain first, second, and third-party validation—getting straight A's in school, helping out in the community, exerting ourselves physically on a team to achieve some external game goal—aren't guaranteed.

Our parental wizards fail us. They are not magical. They are as clueless about the world's ways in as many ways as we are and their worldview will not work for us.

Can you see how this painful, but enlightening, realization is part and parcel of the maturation process? And Dorothy's discovery—that the parental figure she thought would solve her problem is as vulnerable and fallible a person as she is—is the Global Turning Point Progressive Complication of the Story.

It's a point of no return. Dorothy can't "unlearn" the truth about the Wizard of Oz. Now, she has to formulate some plan of her own. She has to figure out her core problem and then develop a slew of tactics to solve it. No one can solve Dorothy's problems but Dorothy.

Many of us, supposed mature adults, still buy into this paradigm, looking for "the magical figure" who will solve our problems for us. I suspect this is why Baum's story crossed the chasm from "fun children's adventure story" into a timeless cross-generational cathartic experience.

No matter how old we are, we often find ourselves ready, willing, and able to turn our agency over to charismatic figures who promise they'll take care of us and bring us back to our "home comforts" when things were stable and straightforward. The thing to remember is we were helpless children back then, not the powerful agentic figures we are today.

The Wonderful Wizard of Oz serves to remind us of that fact.

THE HJ2.0 GLOBAL CRISIS

The Global Crisis is the moment when the protagonist correctly formulates their problem with specificity. As inventor Charles Kettering said, "A problem well stated is a problem half-solved." So, at last, the protagonist applies attention and energy to the Global Inciting Incident's Invisible Phere Gorilla. The result is to understand the Invisible Phere Gorilla represents a problem in the form of a binary choice.

To metabolize and dispel this phenomenon's negative effect, the protagonist reasons they can take "this action" or "that action." This amounts to minimizing the negative (the best bad choice for the protagonist) or a zero-sum calculation of the positive (irreconcilable goods choice, either positive for the protagonist or positive for other agents in their arena, but not both).

Thematically, this moment is the result of directly identifying and correctly categorizing what that Global Inciting Incident, or Invisible Phere Gorilla, introduced at the beginning represents.

The global category of the Invisible Phere Gorilla for an HJ2.0 story boils down to a single existential dilemma. The HJ2.0 Invisible Phere Gorilla is all about dealing with universal chaos, the unexpected drop-ins of change phenomena themselves.

Remember that HJ2.0 shows us how we can best navigate the world when we have no certainty about our navigational system. So, the Invisible Phere Gorilla for an HJ2.0 is all about something that disintegrates the protagonist's existing navigational structure and what the protagonist must do to reform a new, better navigational system to replace it. The new system will be able to cope with this specific category of Invisible Phere Gorillas in the future.

And because the protagonist will have an indelible experience coming out on the other side of traumatic navigational system destruction with a better attunement to the natural world, the protagonist will be better prepared to undergo future worldview upgrades. They can add additional categories of Invisible Phere Gorilla metabolism with less trauma.

The Global Crisis of the HJ2.0, therefore, is a distillation all about coming to terms with uncertainty. It's about recognizing that pursuing a definitive goal state is not why we're here. Instead, the point is to pursue novel meaning not to attain ultimate meaning, which is, by universal first principals, unattainable. When our meaning seems entirely out of our grasp, we need to seek it nevertheless. We must stay the course.

The Crisis of the HJ2.0 is the existential Crisis itself.

If, contrary to all we've held to be real, there is no guarantee of ultimate singular meaning in existence, how is the individual to continue?

The Crisis for the HJ2.0 is contending with the inevitable loss of certainty. Growth requires loss. It requires putting away childish things and recognizing that clinging to certainty is folly when we know so little about life. The wisest among us accept just how little they understand or are capable of understanding.

That revelation is the ultimate metabolization of the Global Inciting Incident of the HJ2.0. In the case of *The Wonderful Wizard of Oz*, the cyclone is a clear externalized instance of environmental chaos that knocks Dorothy into a whole other dimension of time and space. No one can save her from that chaos. It just is.

Coming to terms with the universal truth that some things will knock you out, but you can't see them coming and going on your idiosyncratic mission to survive, thrive, and derive meaning anyway is what the heroic journey is all about. We must go on seeking to derive our meaning on earth, but more importantly, the collective meaning of the species.

Let's view this Crisis in terms of the best bad choice or an irreconcilable goods choice.

Once we surrender to our inability to have final and complete certainty about the universe's nature, is it better to conclude that life is meaningless and thus not care about anything anymore? Or is it better to go on searching for meaning and continue to care, even though there is no guarantee there is any?

That's the best bad choice the protagonist faces, and it's all of ours too.

Let's break the choice down a bit more.

It's better for the species' long-term continuation if every individual member continues to care about creating a meaningful existence even without a guarantee of any ultimate meaning. If we take care, the chances are that our species will survive. For the individual, though, in their short-term life span, it would seem to be better not to care about "meaning" and instead set out to experience more pleasure than pain on earth.

So, what's good for the species comes at the expense of the individual and vice versa.

Can you see how deep the HJ2.0 is? When we distill what Jung identified as the monomyth and what Campbell used to mechanize commercially viable story arcs, we discover an enormously important philosophical paradox.

What's extraordinarily heartening about the HJ2.0 is that there is very little ambiguity about what must be done. The climax is certain and inevitable, not random and uncertain. And we cathartically recognize that certainty as universally true—no matter our first, second, or third-party secular affiliations or the collective cultural grammar of our time.

THE HJ2.0 GLOBAL CRISIS OF THE WONDERFUL WIZARD OF OZ

After the Wizard of Oz recognizes and validates the capabilities of the Scarecrow, the Tin Woodman, and the Lion with symbolic credentials that the characters (and the collective cultural grammar of the magical world) recognize as legitimate, he concocts a plan to attain Dorothy's goal. Thematically, this is the equivalent of a parent desperately trying to rescue their child from chaos even after the child recognizes that parent's inability to do so.

Dorothy's dog Toto, who represents the trickster archetype that nudges protagonists to confront the Invisible Phere Gorillas, runs away again at the critical moment when Dorothy's safety is about to be assured. Remember that Toto was responsible for Dorothy not making it down into the underground shelter at the very beginning of the story. Now Oz flies away in his hot air balloon without Dorothy, and she has, at last, reached her "all-is-lost" moment.

The "all-is-lost" moment is when the protagonist's worldview breaks irrevocably. And soon after that the global Crisis of the HJ2.0 emerges. It's a Samuel Beckett conundrum.

"You must go on. I can't go on. I'll go on." — Samuel Beckett, *The Unnamable*

The global Crisis for the heroic being is simply about whether they ought to go on. It's Hamlet's famous "to be, or not to be" contemplation.

What shall I do when the foundation of what I've held true has proven false?

Dorothy believed to the depths of her cells that the Wizard of Oz was going to solve her problem. Even after he failed her, revealing himself to be a fraud, she still held out hope that he'd be able to think of something to fix it for her. He did, but we'll never know if he was right, just as we'll never know if we're right about our strategies to get back "home."

The critical element in *The Wonderful Wizard of Oz* as a Worldview Maturation story is that Dorothy placed responsibility for her fulfillment on someone else. Not surprisingly, that lack of belief in oneself as a capable agent who is strong enough to formulate and solve one's own problems is the incredibly powerful Invisible Phere Gorilla behind the maturation arc. In other words, this pattern of behavior (relying upon a parent) works for the child but becomes maladaptive for the adult.

Deep down, the audience knows Dorothy must solve her own problems. The fact that the Wizard fails her twice, while a disappointing emotional punch to the audience's solar plexus, is necessary for the story to work. It's difficult to seize our agency, and we allow those who control it many opportunities to prove their worthiness. Thus, Baum intuitively knew that Dorothy would place her faith in Oz even after he failed her the first time.

So, what's the Crisis? Specifically?

Should Dorothy quit her quest to return home, remain in the Emerald City, and make the best of things? Or should she continue to seek a way home? Should she go on?

We can look at these questions through the lens of the best bad choice or a choice between irreconcilable goods.

In terms of the best bad choice, staying at the Emerald City would mean Dorothy will never see her first-party relations again. Even though Dorothy is an orphan, she has an aunt and uncle back home who she's relied upon to survive, thrive, and derive life meaning. To never see them again will sever her from foundational relationships and leave her adrift. But continuing to seek a way home is likely to be an impossible mission. She's in an alternate world, and no one has any idea where Dorothy came from or how to get back. To stubbornly travel with no exact destination other than seeking for seeking's sake is the definition of an uncertain life path. What's the point of such a life if there is no certainty?

In terms of an irreconcilable goods choice, staying at the Emerald City would be positive for her new friends and the local community. Dorothy's knowledge cultivation capacities, especially when combined collectively with Scarecrow, Tin Woodman, and the Lion, are formidable. What would be best for this alternate world would be for Dorothy to stay. But for Dorothy, staying will keep her from pursuing her actuality or fulfilling her potential. She will never know the life she would have had in Kansas or her agency's importance to the *Homo sapiens'* world. What's good for the group, in this case the people of Emerald City, is not good for the individual.

Any way you look at it, this is a severe Crisis.

But Baum doesn't dwell on this Crisis. He doesn't drag out Dorothy's decision, nor does he belabor her friends' disappointed response.

Why?

Because the need to seek and explore the world with the generic "get back home" goal state was a first principle of the period's collective cultural grammar. The novel was published in the United States in 1900 when modernism and progressive sensibilities were threads in the fabric of modern life. Getting back home embodies the sensibility of seeking to abide by the fundamental tenets of civilization and civility. The progressive era was a movement to solve problems from industrialization, urbanization, immigration, and political corruption, to get back "home" to the nation's founding first principles.

The audience at the time would surely have been disappointed if Dorothy gave up. Surrendering to despair and uncertainty, at that time, wouldn't make sense. And today too. Even after the emergence of postmodernism, absurdism, the baffling behaviors of global states and markets worldwide, and the vacuum suck of meaning out of just about every institution we associate with, if Dorothy quit, the audience would feel, deep in their cells, that the story wasn't "right," that it didn't "ring true."

Why? Because the existential necessity of continuing onward into an uncertain future is required for the individual and the species to survive, thrive, and derive. The Crisis of the HJ2.0 is to recognize that the agentic being inside the universal arena must accept the fundamental requirement to, as Samuel Beckett put it, "go on."

That truth was so fully endorsed in Baum's era that few people even considered that Dorothy might bail on her quest to get home. Instead, Baum brings the crew together once again to see if their collective intelligence can figure out a reasonable next step to solve Dorothy's problem.

THE HJ2.0 GLOBAL CLIMAX

In the Global Climax of the HJ2.0, the protagonist summons their trinity of agentic force, what Schopenhauer called "the will to live," Nietzsche called "the will to power," and Kierkegaard and Frankl called "the will to meaning" to solve their perennial problems to survive, thrive, and derive meaning anew.

Or in Beckett's terms, they resolve to "go on."

All of this is to say they do not quit the mission, even though the goal state they aspire to is as far from attainment as one might imagine. The chances of getting what they want are extraordinarily small, but with a revelatory understanding that whether or not they achieve success is not the point, they calmly move forward. They seek for the sake of seeking.

The Climax of the HJ2.0 is not so much about the drama of the protagonist's Crisis decision. The audience knows the protagonist will choose to enter the ultimate arena to contend with the external or internal forces of chaos in the story's ending payoff. That promise is embedded within the structure of the Aristotelian arc. Instead, the Climax of HJ2.0 is about the protagonist's conscious attitude. Thematically, the protagonist has been acting "unconsciously" throughout all of the action until this specific moment in the story. They've been operating under an autonomic worldview 1.0. But in this pivotal moment, they're building a new worldview 2.0 on the fly, awake and in the moment.

The protagonist now has an optimal grip on the fundamental universal truth of *Homo sapiens'* existence—full awareness of our mortality. For lack of a better phrase, we ought to make the most of the time we have here. To bemoan one's inevitable death while all objects, subjects, and the relationships between them shimmer wondrously in front of us is not the best use of one's time.

So, the protagonist now moves forward with a commitment to explore. They'll continue to fire up their trinity of psychic will (to live, to power, to meaning) and see what is around the next corner, knowing full well that they won't know what they'll find.

Can you see how the protagonist is now moving forward purposefully, with a higher attunement to their environment than ever? They are paying attention to what emerges in front of them in real-time rather than following an inaccurate script or map from their past, that old worldview 1.0.

This awakening is the Global Climax of the HJ2.0, and our ancestors homed in on this prescription as the best means to ensure that the individual and collective species survives, thrives, and derives meaning. And we love this prescription. We find it to be so universally true that we can't experience its revelation enough.

I love the Climax of the HJ2.0 because the result of the story is almost beside the point. What happens around the corner must be exciting and ultimately cathartic for the audience, but it's not the takeaway prescription. Catharsis is the resolution of the story, not the climax.

THE HJ2.0 GLOBAL CLIMAX OF THE
WONDERFUL WIZARD OF OZ

The climax of the story unspools in chapter 18, "Away to the South." It begins:

> Dorothy wept bitterly at the passing of her hope to get home to Kansas again; but when she thought it all over she was glad she had not gone up in a balloon. And she also felt sorry at losing Oz, and so did her companions.

These forty-six words represent the whole enchilada of the maturation plot, setting up the ending payoff resolution of this painful but necessary and ultimately sufficient revelation. Baum reveals it in this sentence three-quarters of the way through his story (chapter 18 of 24).

The child who is transforming into an adult must mourn the loss of their reliance upon their parental figures to oversee their development. That's what this first sentence is all about. You'll also notice that Dorothy "thought it all over," which is the critical employment of second-order thinking about one's life events. Her conclusion is surprising, too. "She was glad she had not gone up in a balloon."

What might that mean thematically?

Not to get too metaphorical here, but there is a long tradition that associates death with a soul's ascension. Death is how our authentic being leaves our body and moves upward to a higher realm of eternal consciousness. Oz's choice to ascend away from the Emerald City and his offering the same option to Dorothy could be interpreted as a suicide pact, the quitting of life on the surface. Refusing to "go on."

As Dorothy is still a child at that moment in time, she wholeheartedly agrees to the pact. But then an unexpected, chaotic event drops in, a circumstance beyond her control. Toto's escape just as she was to get in the balloon saves her from that fate.

Now, soon after the catastrophe of losing her last best chance of returning home, she realizes that going up in the balloon would have been a mistake.

This ability to metaphorically step back and contemplate one's life events from an abstract meta-point of view is the mark of the adult. In this one introductory sentence, Baum informs the reader that after Dorothy mourns and cries about her loss, she seizes the potential of her cognitive capacities and thinks about what the event could have meant for her. And she knows now—has the insight—to understand that the balloon and following Oz wasn't the best choice. She now understands that continuing her quest on the surface is a wiser decision than turning over her agency to Oz, who's resolved to live above the surface, at the mercy of phenomena beyond his control.

She must go on. And she must use all her knowledge (propositional, procedural, perspectival, and participatory) to chart her own agentic choices.

The climax sets up the resolution. How exactly will Dorothy move forward in her goal to get back home again?

Wisely, she enlists the help of the creatures in this extraordinary world who know it better than her. She brings together the Scarecrow, the Tin Woodman, and the Lion to figure out a global problem-solving strategy. They'll seek advice from Glinda, the good witch who has already proven her authenticity as a supernatural force. And they'll use a whole toolbox full of tactics (skills that each member of the group possesses independently) to make it to Glinda's home.

THE HJ2.0 GLOBAL RESOLUTION

The Global Resolution of the HJ2.0 is the response to the protagonist's climactic action from the environment. It's what the world and the beings around the protagonist do in response to their applying their agentic self.

The idea behind the resolution is that agents' actions are processed and metabolized by the universal arena, which includes the ecological and socio-cultural environments (the relationships between the agents in the arena in the collective cultural milieu). We are embedded inside the system, not players outside the system. In the same way, no cell in a being's body is independent of the cells and structures surrounding it, nor is the individual independent from the beings and systems that surround them.

The response from the universal arena could cause the protagonist's physical death. They take an action that results in the environment or one of the other agents in their arena taking their life. The being's body ceases to be animate, and any of their future potential agentic actions that their body could have employed vanish with the body's dissolution.

Physical death, however, is not sufficient to ensure metaphysical death. Depending upon the meaning the being was creating at the time of their physical death (the qualities of the active assertion of their agentic capacity, or what they "meant"), the being could live on in the minds of those they left behind. Those minds include their first-party relationships, their second-party tribal affiliations, and even up to third-party mass populations. Historical figures like Joan of Arc, Siddhartha Gautama, and Martin Luther King, Jr. come to mind as beings who are more metaphysically potent and alive today than when they were physical actors on the earth.

While our bodies have natural and context-specific expiration dates, our metaphysical meanings are under no such constraints. They can live far longer in the imaginations of our fellow beings' minds than can our objectively documented earthly interactions.

But wait, there's more.

Joan of Arc was a once in a millennia kind of historical figure. What can the average *Homo sapiens* do to create lasting metaphysical meaning?

Our interactions indeed have linear limitations. An individual can only have authentic interaction with so many fellow *Homo sapiens* in their lifetime.

But our creations, the psycho-technologies and technologies that only we could introduce in the world, can prove to be adaptively advantageous for our entire species through time. And those creations can serve as our legacy. Forget the inaccurate symbolic representations of us like those we think of when we think of historical figures. We'll never really know or understand the authentic people behind those historical representations.

Instead, consider the first *Homo sapiens* who had the imagination and courage to drape an arm across one of their fellow beings and squeeze them to reassure them that they understood what the other person was experiencing. Let them know that they got just how damn hard it was to navigate this world and that their suffering hadn't gone unnoticed. That intimate creation proved magical.

Today, we have no idea who that individual was. They didn't "get credit" for their innovative firm shoulder hug technology. Does it matter? The creation that came from their mind is so thoroughly incorporated into what it means to be human now that it's immortal. I suspect that inventive being is peacefully resting somewhere, even though, and mainly because, no one knows who they are.

What does this have to do with the Resolution of the Heroic Journey 2.0?

The resolution not only shows the reaction from the ecological and socio-cultural environment in terms of physics (whether the protagonist's body survives) but also is the explication of the metaphysical meaning of the story (what the protagonist's death or survival means).

Whether the protagonist survives the physical circumstances of their agentic choices isn't as important as the clarity of the metaphysical legacy of their choice to "go on." If they die, the embedded HJ2.0 meaning is *at least they tried to carry on and to help others carry on in their unique way too.*

Their going on in their seeking of personal and collective truth despite the effects on their physical being (their suffering and pain) is the whole point of the HJ2.0.

Going on and continuing to search for meaning and truth is what we must do as individual *Homo sapiens* to continue to create adaptive advantages for the entire species, now and into the future. These adaptive advantages (symbolic representations of the necessity for us to pursue meaning and truth and the literal "story" the storytelling creator offers to the species) are our only hope to forestall termination of our species.

That may sound overly dramatic, but when one reads and analyzes hundreds of stories at multiple macro and micro levels (as Jung, Campbell, and I have), the clarity of that meta-monomythic ancestral tone booms true.

So right and real that it feels like it's a "duh, of course, that's what it's all about" kind of revelatory phenomenon.

THE HJ2.0 GLOBAL RESOLUTION OF THE WONDERFUL WIZARD OF OZ

I confess that I wasn't all that enthralled with *The Wonderful Wizard of Oz* as a kid or even as recently as last year. That isn't to say I haven't read it several times in my lifetime. I've seen the movie adaptation about twenty times too. It was a Thanksgiving tradition for our family for years, until sadly, the rest of the family weren't so into it anymore.

But now, after having re-read and analyzed the story with high-resolution micro and macro detail, I see why it continues to be such an essential contribution to our collective cultural grammar.

It's just so fundamentally accurate about how difficult it is to become an adult, remain an adult, and die with an adult's dignity. It works at any level of one's maturity. And thankfully, we're all in the process of leveling up our cognitive capacities (maturing) until the very last breath we take.

That's what the HJ2.0 is encouraging us to do—to grow, mature, and commit oneself to the search process for truth, even though we know we'll never find a single answer. The universal arena is always changing, which requires that we change too. Then our changes feed back into the system to change the arena yet again. There is no final truth, only the creative act of meaning-making in the context of the here and now.

So how does *The Wonderful Wizard of Oz* resolve?

Dorothy, the Scarecrow, the Tin Woodman, and the Lion assert their agentic capabilities together to solve the fundamental problem posed by the story's Global Inciting Incident—the cyclone back in Kansas that serves as the Invisible Phere Gorilla.

It's worth unpacking that a bit. Remember that the beginning of the story began on earth, in Kansas. And a random environmental event occurred that transported Dorothy to an alternate world. That was the cyclone. So, suppose we're thinking about the kind of damage a cyclone could inflict on an immature person. We can reasonably assume that Dorothy was knocked unconscious because she did not make it into the underground shelter.

So, the entire story takes us inside Dorothy's mind. She's "asleep," navigating her unconscious world. What's thematically brilliant is that Dorothy will not be able to go home again in her mind until she physically awakens. So, her motor actions on earth cannot come back online until she has metaphysical enlightenment.

The cyclone is the random vector/force that demands Dorothy's maturation. Can you see why it's an Invisible Phere Gorilla? Dorothy will have no idea that she's been knocked unconscious by an external force (the cyclone is invisible to her in her unconscious mind) until she is mature enough to awaken to the reality of an adult's understanding that you don't see some things coming that will knock you out.

So, how does Baum resolve the story?

The ending payoff takes quite some time to conclude because Baum wants to show these four committed agents working together to solve a single problem. Plus, their behavior isn't all positive either. These beings inflict some serious second-order effects upon their environment as they navigate to Glinda the Good Witch's house.

After disrupting several ecosystems on the way (you see how agents are strong forces of change in and of themselves), the group reaches Glinda.

Dorothy asks for Glinda's help.

Why is this plea different than her requests for help from Oz? Because Dorothy, while she has hope that Glinda will help, hasn't surrendered her agency in the way that she previously had with Oz. She used to think that an appeal to an authority figure with all the right credentials would result in a sure solution to her problem. She still seeks those who have more information and more knowledge than she does, but now she has not staked all her confidence in that figure's ability to help her. She's consulting with rather than relying upon an authority.

What Glinda reveals to her, after she tests Dorothy's trust by asking for her magic cap, is that Dorothy has had the capability all along to return home. All she has to do is command her silver shoes (shoes are the tools we put on our feet to navigate through the world safely) to take her there. Essentially, she must use her mind to engage the motor actions necessary to reach her goal state. In other words, she must think.

And like magic, after Dorothy summons the will to command her shoes, she wakes up, returned to Kansas, a capable agent ready to navigate the rest of her life.

After overcoming the cyclone trauma, Dorothy now has a story to keep her moving forward when random obstacles obstruct her path in the future.

THE HJ2.0 CHEAT SHEET

The Heroic Journey 2.0 consists of five essential elements:

1. The Global Inciting Incident is a worldview destroying Invisible Phere Gorilla.
2. The Global Turning Point Progressive Complication arrives approximately halfway through the story when the protagonist's worldview 1.0 shatters, sending them into utter chaotic confusion.
3. The Global Crisis of the story emerges just after the protagonist realizes that all they held to be true in their past is now lost (the "all-is-lost" moment), from which emerges the mother of all crises, "Should I keep going, keep trying to find the truth? Or should I quit and surrender to nothingness?"
4. The Global Climax of the story is when the protagonist activates their Crisis choice. They *go on* (a prescriptive heroic journey) or *quit* (a cautionary anti-heroic journey).
5. The Global Resolution of the story is the result of the climactic choice. The prescriptive heroic journey pays off with meaning while the cautionary anti-heroic journey pays off with meaninglessness.

INTRODUCTION FROM THE AUTHOR L. FRANK BAUM

Folklore, legends, myths and fairy tales have followed childhood through the ages, for every healthy youngster has a wholesome and instinctive love for stories fantastic, marvelous and manifestly unreal. The winged fairies of Grimm and Andersen have brought more happiness to childish hearts than all other human creations.

Yet the old time fairy tale, having served for generations, may now be classed as "historical" in the children's library; for the time has come for a series of newer "wonder tales" in which the stereotyped genie, dwarf and fairy are eliminated, together with all the horrible and blood-curdling incidents devised by their authors to point a fearsome moral to each tale. Modern education includes morality; therefore the modern child seeks only entertainment in its wonder tales and gladly dispenses with all disagreeable incident.

Having this thought in mind, the story of "The Wonderful Wizard of Oz" was written solely to please children of today. It aspires to being a modernized fairy tale, in which the wonderment and joy are retained and the heartaches and nightmares are left out.

L. Frank Baum
Chicago, April, 1900.

1

THE CYCLONE

SCENE 1

Dorothy lived in the midst of the great Kansas prairies, with **Uncle Henry**, who was a farmer, and **Aunt Em**, who was the farmer's wife. Their house was small, for the lumber to build it had to be carried by wagon many miles. There were four walls, a floor and a roof, which made one room; and this room contained a rusty looking cookstove, a cupboard for the dishes, a table, three or four chairs, and the beds. Uncle Henry and Aunt Em had a big bed in one corner, and Dorothy a little bed in another corner. There was no garret at all, and no cellar— except a small hole dug in the ground, called a cyclone cellar, where the family could go in case one of those great whirlwinds arose, mighty enough to crush any building in its path. It was reached by a trap door in the middle of the floor, from which a ladder led down into the small, dark hole.

When Dorothy stood in the doorway and looked around, she could see nothing but the great **gray prairie** on every side. Not a tree nor a house broke the broad sweep of flat country that reached to the edge of the sky in all directions. The sun had baked the plowed land into a **gray mass**, with little **cracks running through it**. Even the grass was not green, for the sun had burned the tops of the long blades until they were the same **gray color** to be seen everywhere. Once the house had been painted, but the sun blistered the paint and the rains washed it away, and now **the house was as dull and gray as everything else.**

When Aunt Em came there to live she was a young, pretty wife. The sun and wind had changed her, too. They had taken the sparkle from her eyes and left them **a sober gray**; they had taken the red from her cheeks and lips, and **they were gray also.** She was thin and gaunt, and never smiled now. When Dorothy, who was **an orphan,** first came to her, Aunt Em had been so startled by the child's laughter that she would scream and press her hand upon her heart whenever Dorothy's merry voice reached her ears; and she still looked at the little girl with wonder that she could find anything to laugh at.

Uncle Henry never laughed. He worked hard from morning till night and did not know what joy was. **He was gray also,** from his long beard to his rough boots, and he looked stern and solemn, and rarely spoke.

It was **Toto** that made Dorothy laugh, and saved her from growing as gray as her other surroundings. **Toto was not gray**; he was a little black dog, with long silky hair and small black eyes that twinkled merrily on either side of his funny, wee nose. Toto played all day long, and Dorothy played with him, and loved him dearly.

Today, however, they were not playing. Uncle Henry sat upon the doorstep and looked anxiously at the sky, which was even grayer than usual. Dorothy stood in the door with Toto in her arms, and looked at the sky too. Aunt Em was washing the dishes.

From the far north they heard a low wail of the wind, and Uncle Henry and Dorothy could see where the long grass bowed in waves before the coming storm. There now came a sharp whistling in the air from the south, and as they turned their eyes that way they saw ripples in the grass coming from that direction also.

Suddenly Uncle Henry stood up.

"There's a cyclone coming, Em," he called to his wife. "I'll go look after the stock." Then he ran toward the sheds where the cows and horses were kept.

Aunt Em dropped her work and came to the door. One glance told her of the danger close at hand.

"Quick, Dorothy!" she screamed. "Run for the cellar!"

Toto jumped out of Dorothy's arms and hid under the bed, and the girl started to get him. Aunt Em, badly frightened, threw open the trap door in the floor and climbed down the ladder into the small, dark hole. Dorothy caught Toto at last and started to follow her aunt. When she was halfway across the room there came a great shriek from the wind, and the house shook so hard that she lost her footing and sat down suddenly upon the floor.

Then a strange thing happened.

The house whirled around two or three times and rose slowly through the air. Dorothy felt as if she were going up in a balloon.

The north and south winds met where the house stood, and made it the exact center of the cyclone. In the middle of a cyclone the air is generally still, but the great pressure of the wind on every side of the house raised it up higher and higher, until it was at the very top of the cyclone; and there it remained and was carried miles and miles away as easily as you could carry a feather.

It was very dark, and the wind howled horribly around her, but Dorothy found she was riding quite easily. After the first few whirls around, and one other time when the house tipped badly, she felt as if she were being rocked gently, like a baby in a cradle.

Toto did not like it. He ran about the room, now here, now there, barking loudly; but Dorothy sat quite still on the floor and waited to see what would happen.

Once Toto got too near the open trap door, and fell in; and at first the little girl thought she had lost him. But soon she saw one of his ears sticking up through the hole, for the strong pressure of the air was keeping him up so that he could not fall. She crept to the hole, caught Toto by the ear, and dragged him into the room again, afterward closing the trap door so that no more accidents could happen.

Hour after hour passed away, and slowly Dorothy got over her fright; but she felt quite lonely, and the wind shrieked so loudly all about her that she nearly became deaf. At first she had wondered if she would be dashed to pieces when the house fell again; but as the hours passed and nothing terrible happened, she stopped worrying and resolved to wait calmly and see what the future would bring. At last she crawled over the swaying floor to her bed, and lay down upon it; and Toto followed and lay down beside her.

In spite of the swaying of the house and the wailing of the wind, Dorothy soon closed her eyes and fell fast asleep.

• ANALYZING THE SCENE •

STORY EVENT

A Story Event is an active change of a universal human value for one or more characters as a result of conflict (one character's desires clash with another's, or an environmental shift changes the value positively or negatively).

A Working Scene contains at least one Story Event. To determine a scene's Story Event, answer these four Socratic questions:

1. The Action Story Component: What are the characters literally doing—that is, what are their micro on-the-surface actions?

Uncle Henry, Dorothy, and Auntie Em see an impending cyclone and prepare for its arrival.

2. The Worldview Story Component: What is the essential tactic of the characters—that is, what above-the-surface macro behaviors are they employing that are linked to a universal human value?

Uncle Henry safeguards the livestock, Dorothy safeguards Toto, and Auntie Em safeguards herself.

3. The Heroic Journey 2.0 Component: What beyond-the-surface universal human values have changed for one or more characters in the scene? Which one of those value changes is most important and should be included in the Story Grid Spreadsheet?

All the characters' lives are threatened. The value changes from life to possible death for all of them.

Identifying the most important value change in a scene is sometimes difficult. This scene begins on the ground and ends, quite literally, in the air, which threatens the life of the protagonist. So the choice is clear. We'll track "Life to Death" in the value shift column of the spreadsheet.

5

When in doubt, the Story Grid rule of thumb is to highlight the value that best aligns with the progress of the global human value at stake in the story. *The Wonderful Wizard of Oz* is an Action Story, which has a global value at stake of Life/Death. Throughout the Story Grid Spreadsheet, we'll track the ways life is threatened or enhanced scene by scene.

Life to Death

4. The Scene Event Synthesis: What Story Event sums up the scene's on-the-surface actions, essential above-the-surface worldview behavioral tactics, and beyond-the-surface value change? We will enter that event in the Story Grid Spreadsheet.

A cyclone lifts a one-room Kansas farmhouse off of the ground with a little orphan girl and her dog still inside.

HOW THE SCENE ABIDES BY THE FIVE COMMANDMENTS OF STORYTELLING

Inciting Incident: A cyclone approaches a one-room farmhouse on the wide-open Kansas plains.

Turning Point Progressive Complication: Toto the dog leaps from Dorothy's arms as she moves toward the cellar door. Toto's unexpected disobedience is the active turn in the story that changes the universal human value from safe and alive to in danger and close to death.

Crisis: Best bad choice. If Dorothy turns back to fetch Toto, she will likely endanger herself. If she doesn't, Toto is certain to die.

Climax: Dorothy rescues Toto.

Resolution: The farmhouse is lifted off the ground by the cyclone with Dorothy and Toto still inside.

2

THE COUNCIL WITH THE MUNCHKINS

SCENE 2

She was awakened by a shock, so sudden and severe that if **Dorothy** had not been lying on the soft bed she might have been hurt. As it was, the jar made her catch her breath and wonder what had happened; and **Toto** put his cold little nose into her face and whined dismally. Dorothy sat up and noticed that the house was not moving; nor was it dark, for the **bright sunshine came in at the window**, flooding the little room. She sprang from her bed and with Toto at her heels ran and opened the door.

The little girl gave a cry of amazement and looked about her, her eyes growing bigger and bigger at the wonderful sights she saw.

The cyclone had set the house down very gently—for a cyclone—**in the midst of a country of marvelous beauty.** There were lovely patches of greensward all about, with stately trees bearing rich and luscious fruits. Banks of gorgeous flowers were on every hand, and birds with rare and brilliant plumage sang and fluttered in the trees and bushes. A little way off was a small brook, rushing and sparkling along between green banks, and murmuring in a voice very grateful to a little girl who had lived so long on **the dry, gray prairies.**

While she stood looking eagerly at the strange and beautiful sights, she noticed coming toward her **a group of the queerest people she had ever seen**. They were not as big as the grown folk she had always been used to; but neither were they very small. In fact, they seemed about as tall as Dorothy, who was a well-grown child for her age, although they were, so far as looks go, many years older.

Three were men and one a woman, and all were oddly dressed. They wore round hats that rose to a small point a foot above their heads, with little bells around the brims that tinkled sweetly as they moved. The hats of the men were blue; the little woman's hat was white, and she wore a white gown that hung in pleats from her shoulders. Over it were sprinkled little stars that glistened in the sun like diamonds. The men were dressed in blue, of the same shade as their hats, and wore well-polished boots with a deep roll of blue at the tops. The men, Dorothy thought, were about as old as Uncle Henry, for two of them had beards. But the little woman was doubtless much older. Her face was covered with wrinkles, her hair was nearly white, and she walked rather stiffly.

When these people drew near the house where Dorothy was standing in the doorway, they paused and whispered among themselves, as if afraid to come farther. But the little old woman walked up to Dorothy, made a low bow and said, in a sweet voice:

"You are welcome, most noble Sorceress, to the **land of the Munchkins**. We are so grateful to you for having killed the **Wicked Witch of the East**, and for setting our people free from bondage."

Dorothy listened to this speech with wonder. What could the little woman possibly mean by calling her a sorceress, and saying she had killed the Wicked Witch of the East? Dorothy was an innocent, harmless little girl, who had been carried by a cyclone many miles from home; and she had never killed anything in all her life.

But the little woman evidently expected her to answer; so Dorothy said, with hesitation, "You are very kind, but there must be some mistake. I have not killed anything."

"Your house did, anyway," replied the little old woman, with a laugh, "and that is the same thing. See!" she continued, pointing to the corner of the house. "There are her two feet, still sticking out from under a block of wood."

8

Dorothy looked, and gave a little cry of fright. There, indeed, just under the corner of the great beam the house rested on, two feet were sticking out, shod in **silver shoes with pointed toes.**

"Oh, dear! Oh, dear!" cried Dorothy, clasping her hands together in dismay. "The house must have fallen on her. Whatever shall we do?"

"There is nothing to be done," said the little woman calmly.

"But who was she?" asked Dorothy.

"She was the Wicked Witch of the East, as I said," answered the little woman. "She has held all the Munchkins in bondage for many years, making them slave for her night and day. Now they are all set free, and are grateful to you for the favor."

"Who are the Munchkins?" inquired Dorothy.

"They are the people who live in this land of the East where the Wicked Witch ruled."

"Are you a Munchkin?" asked Dorothy.

"No, but I am their friend, although I live in the land of the North. When they saw the Witch of the East was dead the Munchkins sent a swift messenger to me, and I came at once. I am the Witch of the North."

"Oh, gracious!" cried Dorothy. "Are you a real witch?"

"Yes, indeed," answered the little woman. "But I am a good witch, and the people love me. I am not as powerful as the Wicked Witch was who ruled here, or I should have set the people free myself."

"But I thought all witches were wicked," said the girl, who was half frightened at facing a real witch. "Oh, no, that is a great mistake. There were only four witches in all the Land of Oz, and two of them, those who live in the North and the South, are good witches. I know this is true, for I am one of them myself, and cannot be mistaken. Those who dwelt in the East and the West were, indeed, wicked witches; but now that you have killed one of them, there is but one **Wicked Witch in all the Land of Oz—the one who lives in the West.**"

"But," said Dorothy, after a moment's thought, "**Aunt Em** has told me that the witches were all dead—years and years ago."

"Who is Aunt Em?" inquired the little old woman.

"She is my aunt who lives in Kansas, where I came from."

The Witch of the North seemed to think for a time, with her head bowed and her eyes upon the ground. Then she looked up and said, "I do not know where Kansas is, for I have never heard that country mentioned before. But tell me, is it a civilized country?"

"Oh, yes," replied Dorothy.

"Then that accounts for it. In the civilized countries I believe there are no witches left, nor wizards, nor sorceresses, nor magicians. But, you see, **the Land of Oz has never been civilized, for we are cut off from all the rest of the world. Therefore we still have witches and wizards amongst us.**"

"Who are the wizards?" asked Dorothy.

"Oz himself is the Great Wizard," answered the Witch, sinking her voice to a whisper. "He is more powerful than all the rest of us together. He lives in the City of Emeralds."

Dorothy was going to ask another question, but just then the Munchkins, who had been standing silently by, gave a loud shout and pointed to the corner of the house where the Wicked Witch had been lying.

"What is it?" asked the little old woman, and looked, and began to laugh. The feet of the dead Witch had disappeared entirely, and nothing was left but the silver shoes.

"She was so old," explained the Witch of the North, "that she dried up quickly in the sun. That is the end of her. But the silver shoes are yours, and you shall have them to wear." She reached down and picked up the shoes, and after shaking the dust out of them handed them to Dorothy.

"The Witch of the East was proud of those silver shoes," said one of the Munchkins, "and there is some charm connected with them; but what it is we never knew."

Dorothy carried the shoes into the house and placed them on the table. Then she came out again to the Munchkins and said:

"I am anxious to get back to my aunt and uncle, for I am sure they will worry about me. Can you help me find my way?"

The Munchkins and the Witch first looked at one another, and then at Dorothy, and then shook their heads.

"At the East, not far from here," said one, "there is a great desert, and none could live to cross it."

"It is the same at the South," said another, "for I have been there and seen it. The South is the country of the Quadlings."

"I am told," said the third man, "that it is the same at the West. And that country, where the Winkies live, is ruled by the Wicked Witch of the West, who would make you her slave if you passed her way."

"The North is my home," said the old lady, "and at its edge is the same great desert that surrounds this Land of Oz. I'm afraid, my dear, you will have to live with us."

Dorothy began to sob at this, for she felt lonely among all these strange people. Her tears seemed to grieve the kind-hearted Munchkins, for they immediately took out their handkerchiefs and began to weep also. As for the little old woman, she took off her cap and balanced the point on the end of her nose, while she counted "One, two, three" in a solemn voice. At once the cap changed to a slate, on which was written in big, white chalk marks:

"LET DOROTHY GO TO THE CITY OF EMERALDS"

The little old woman took the slate from her nose, and having read the words on it, asked, "Is your name Dorothy, my dear?"

"Yes," answered the child, looking up and drying her tears.

"Then you must go to the City of Emeralds. Perhaps Oz will help you."

"Where is this city?" asked Dorothy.

"It is exactly in the center of the country, and is ruled by Oz, the Great Wizard I told you of."

"Is he a good man?" inquired the girl anxiously.

"He is a good Wizard. Whether he is a man or not I cannot tell, for I have never seen him."

"How can I get there?" asked Dorothy.

"You must walk. It is a long journey, through a country that is sometimes pleasant and sometimes dark and terrible. However, I will use all the magic arts I know of to keep you from harm."

"Won't you go with me?" pleaded the girl, who had begun to look upon the little old woman as her only friend.

"No, I cannot do that," she replied, "but I will give you my kiss, and no one will dare injure a person who has been kissed by the Witch of the North."

She came close to Dorothy and kissed her gently on the forehead. Where her lips touched the girl they left a round, shining mark, as Dorothy found out soon after.

"The road to the City of Emeralds is paved with yellow brick," said the Witch, "so you cannot miss it. When you get to Oz do not be afraid of him, but tell your story and ask him to help you. Good-bye, my dear."

The three Munchkins bowed low to her and wished her a pleasant journey, after which they walked away through the trees. The Witch gave Dorothy a friendly little nod, whirled around on her left heel three times, and straightway disappeared, much to the surprise of little Toto, who barked after her loudly enough when she had gone, because he had been afraid even to growl while she stood by.

But Dorothy, knowing her to be a witch, had expected her to disappear in just that way, and was not surprised in the least.

• ANALYZING THE SCENE •

STORY EVENT

A Story Event is an active change of a universal human value for one or more characters as a result of conflict (one character's desires clash with another's, or an environmental shift changes the universal human value).

A Working Scene contains at least one Story Event. To determine a scene's Story Event, answer these four Socratic questions:

1. The Action Story Component: What are the characters literally doing—that is, what are their micro on-the-surface actions?

Dorothy and Toto's house falls atop the Wicked Witch of the East in the land of the Munchkins. They are then greeted by a woman and three small men who inform them of where they are.

2. The Worldview Story Component: What is the essential tactic of the characters—that is, what above-the-surface macro behaviors are they employing that are linked to a universal human value?

Dorothy asks for advice about getting home to Kansas.

3. The Heroic Journey 2.0 Component: What beyond-the-surface universal human values have changed for one or more characters in the scene? Which one of those value changes is most important and should be included in the Story Grid Spreadsheet?

Dorothy has survived the cyclone but is far from home with no clue about how to get back to Kansas. Then the Good Witch of the South advises her to follow the yellow brick road to the City of Emeralds and meet with the Wizard of Oz. Her universal human values shift from "Safe to Lost to Directed."

The Munchkins and the Good Witch of the South are overjoyed by the death of the Wicked Witch of the East. They greet Dorothy, who they believe is a sorceress responsible for the Munchkin liberation but are at a loss about how to repay her until the Good Witch seeks supernatural counsel. Their universal human values shift from "Overjoyed to Frustrated to Relieved."

When in doubt, the Story Grid rule of thumb is to highlight the value that best aligns with the progress of the global human value at stake in the story. *The Wonderful Wizard of Oz* is an Action Story, which has a global value at stake of Life/Death. Throughout the Story Grid Spreadsheet, we'll track the ways life is threatened or enhanced scene by scene.

As Dorothy is the protagonist and her life is enhanced by her shift of universal human value in this scene, we'll track her value shift.

Safe to Lost to Directed

4. The Scene Event Synthesis: What Story Event sums up the scene's on-the-surface actions, essential above-the-surface worldview behavioral tactics, and beyond-the-surface value change? We will enter that event in the Story Grid Spreadsheet.

Dorothy drops into the Land of the Munchkins and asks and receives advice about how to begin navigating back home.

HOW THE SCENE ABIDES BY THE FIVE COMMANDMENTS OF STORYTELLING

Inciting Incident: Dorothy's house lands on the Wicked Witch of the East, safeguarding the lives of those living in the Land of the Munchkins.

Turning Point Progressive Complication: The Land of the Munchkins is far, far away from Kansas. The Good Witch of the South asks the universe about what Dorothy should do and receives the message that Dorothy should go to the Emerald City.

Crisis: Best bad choice. If Dorothy stays in the Land of the Munchkins, she'll never see her uncle or aunt again. If she sets off to go home, she could lose herself forever, as the country she must traverse is often dark and terrible.

Climax: Dorothy resolves to take the advice of the Good Witch of the South, follow the yellow brick road to the City of Emeralds and ask the Wizard of Oz for help getting home.

Resolution: The Good Witch of the South gives Dorothy a kiss to protect her on her journey.

3
HOW DOROTHY SAVED THE SCARECROW

SCENE 3

When **Dorothy** was left alone she began to feel hungry. So she went to the cupboard and cut herself some bread, which she spread with butter. She gave some to **Toto**, and taking a pail from the shelf she carried it down to the little brook and filled it with clear, sparkling water. Toto ran over to the trees and began to bark at the birds sitting there. Dorothy went to get him, and saw such delicious fruit hanging from the branches that she gathered some of it, finding it just what she wanted to help out her breakfast.

Then she went back to the house, and having helped herself and Toto to a good drink of the cool, clear water, she set about making ready for the journey to the City of Emeralds.

Dorothy had only one other dress, but that happened to be clean and was hanging on a peg beside her bed. It was gingham, with checks of white and blue; and although the blue was somewhat faded with many washings, it was still a pretty frock. The girl washed herself carefully, dressed herself in the clean gingham, and tied her pink sunbonnet on her head. She took a little basket and filled it with bread from the cupboard, laying a white cloth over the top. Then she looked down at her feet and noticed how old and worn her shoes were.

"They surely will never do for a long journey, Toto," she said. And Toto looked up into her face with his little black eyes and wagged his tail to show he knew what she meant.

At that moment Dorothy saw lying on the table the silver shoes that had belonged to **the Witch of the East.**

"I wonder if they will fit me," she said to Toto. "They would be just the thing to take a long walk in, for they could not wear out."

She took off her old leather shoes and tried on the silver ones, which fitted her as well as if they had been made for her.

Finally she picked up her basket.

"Come along, Toto," she said. "We will go to the Emerald City and ask **the Great Oz** how to get back to Kansas again."

She closed the door, locked it, and put the key carefully in the pocket of her dress. And so, with Toto trotting along soberly behind her, she started on her journey.

There were several roads nearby, but it did not take her long to find the one paved with yellow bricks. Within a short time she was walking briskly toward the Emerald City, her silver shoes tinkling merrily on the hard, yellow road-bed. The sun shone bright and the birds sang sweetly, and Dorothy did not feel nearly so bad as you might think a little girl would who had been suddenly whisked away from her own country and set down in the midst of a strange land.

She was surprised, as she walked along, to see **how pretty the country was about her. There were neat fences at the sides of the road, painted a dainty blue color, and beyond them were fields of grain and vegetables in abundance. Evidently the Munchkins were good farmers and able to raise large crops. Once in a while she would pass a house, and the people came out to look at her and bow low as she went by; for everyone knew she had been the means of destroying the Wicked Witch and setting them free from bondage. The houses of the Munchkins were odd-looking dwellings, for each was round, with a big dome for a roof. All were painted blue, for in this country of the East blue was the favorite color.**

Toward evening, when Dorothy was tired with her long walk and began to wonder where she should pass the night, she came to a house rather larger than the rest. On the green lawn before it many men and women were dancing. Five little fiddlers played as loudly as possible, and the people were laughing and singing, while a big table near by was loaded with delicious fruits and nuts, pies and cakes, and many other good things to eat.

The people greeted Dorothy kindly, and invited her to supper and to pass the night with them; for this was the home of one of the richest Munchkins in the land, and his friends were gathered with him to celebrate their freedom from the bondage of the Wicked Witch.

Dorothy ate a hearty supper and was waited upon by the rich Munchkin himself, whose name was Boq. Then she sat upon a settee and watched the people dance.

When Boq saw her silver shoes he said, "You must be a great sorceress."

"Why?" asked the girl.

"Because you wear silver shoes and have killed the Wicked Witch. Besides, you have white in your frock, and only witches and sorceresses wear white."

"My dress is blue and white checked," said Dorothy, smoothing out the wrinkles in it.

"It is kind of you to wear that," said Boq. **Blue is the color of the Munchkins, and white is the witch color. So we know you are a friendly witch.**

Dorothy did not know what to say to this, for all the people seemed to think her a witch, and she knew very well she was only an ordinary little girl who had come by the chance of a cyclone into a strange land.

When she had tired watching the dancing, Boq led her into the house, where he gave her a room with a pretty bed in it. The sheets were made of blue cloth, and Dorothy slept soundly in them till morning, with Toto curled up on the blue rug beside her.

She ate a hearty breakfast, and watched a wee Munchkin baby, who played with Toto and pulled his tail and crowed and laughed in a way that greatly amused Dorothy. Toto was a fine curiosity to all the people, for they had never seen a dog before.

"How far is it to the Emerald City?" the girl asked.

"I do not know," answered Boq gravely, "for I have never been there. It is better for people to keep away from Oz, unless they have business with him. But it is a long way to the Emerald City, and it will take you many days. **The country here is rich and pleasant, but you must pass through rough and dangerous places before you reach the end of your journey.**"

This worried Dorothy a little, but she knew that only the Great Oz could help her get to Kansas again, so she bravely resolved not to turn back.

She bade her friends good-bye, and again started along the road of yellow brick. When she had gone several miles she thought she would stop to rest, and so climbed to the top of the fence beside the road and sat down. There was a great cornfield beyond the fence, and not far away she saw **a Scarecrow**, placed high on a pole to keep the birds from the ripe corn.

Dorothy leaned her chin upon her hand and gazed thoughtfully at the Scarecrow. Its head was a small sack stuffed with straw, with eyes, nose, and mouth painted on it to represent a face. An old, pointed blue hat, that had belonged to some Munchkin, was perched on his head, and the rest of the figure was a blue suit of clothes, worn and faded, which had also been stuffed with straw. On the feet were some old boots with blue tops, such as every man wore in this country, and the figure was raised above the stalks of corn by means of the pole stuck up its back.

While Dorothy was looking earnestly into the queer, painted face of the Scarecrow, she was surprised to see one of the eyes slowly wink at her. She thought she must have been mistaken at first, for none of the scarecrows in Kansas ever wink; but presently the figure nodded its head to her in a friendly way. Then she climbed down from the fence and walked up to it, while Toto ran around the pole and barked.

"Good day," said the Scarecrow, in a rather husky voice.

"Did you speak?" asked the girl, in wonder.

"Certainly," answered the Scarecrow. "How do you do?"

"I'm pretty well, thank you," replied Dorothy politely. "How do you do?"

"I'm not feeling well," said the Scarecrow, with a smile, "for it is very tedious being perched up here night and day to scare away crows."

"Can't you get down?" asked Dorothy.

"No, for this pole is stuck up my back. If you will please take away the pole I shall be greatly obliged to you."

Dorothy reached up both arms and lifted the figure off the pole, for, being stuffed with straw, it was quite light.

"Thank you very much," said the Scarecrow, when he had been set down on the ground. "I feel like a new man."

Dorothy was puzzled at this, for it sounded queer to hear a stuffed man speak, and to see him bow and walk along beside her.

"Who are you?" asked the Scarecrow when he had stretched himself and yawned. "And where are you going?"

"My name is Dorothy," said the girl, "and I am going to the Emerald City, to ask the Great Oz to send me back to Kansas."

"Where is the Emerald City?" he inquired. "And who is Oz?"

"Why, don't you know?" she returned, in surprise.

"No, indeed. I don't know anything. You see, I am stuffed, so I have no brains at all," he answered sadly.

"Oh," said Dorothy, "I'm awfully sorry for you."

"Do you think," he asked, "if I go to the Emerald City with you, that Oz would give me some brains?"

"I cannot tell," she returned, "but you may come with me, if you like. If Oz will not give you any brains you will be no worse off than you are now."

"That is true," said the Scarecrow. "You see," he continued confidentially, **"I don't mind my legs and arms and body being stuffed, because I cannot get hurt. If anyone treads on my toes or sticks a pin into me, it doesn't matter, for I can't feel it. But I do not want people to call me a fool, and if my head stays stuffed with straw instead of with brains, as yours is, how am I ever to know anything?"**

"I understand how you feel," said the little girl, who was truly sorry for him. "If you will come with me I'll ask Oz to do all he can for you."

"Thank you," he answered gratefully.

They walked back to the road. Dorothy helped him over the fence, and they started along the path of yellow brick for the Emerald City.

Toto did not like this addition to the party at first. He smelled around the stuffed man as if he suspected there might be a nest of rats in the straw, and he often growled in an unfriendly way at the Scarecrow.

"Don't mind Toto," said Dorothy to her new friend. "He never bites."

"Oh, I'm not afraid," replied the Scarecrow. "He can't hurt the straw. Do let me carry that basket for you. I shall not mind it, for I can't get tired. I'll tell you a secret," he continued, as he walked along. "There is only one thing in the world I am afraid of."

"What is that?" asked Dorothy; "the Munchkin farmer who made you?"

"No," answered the Scarecrow; "it's a lighted match."

• ANALYZING THE SCENE •

STORY EVENT

A Story Event is an active change of a universal human value for one or more characters as a result of conflict (one character's desires clash with another's, or an environmental shift changes the universal human value).

A Working Scene contains at least one Story Event. To determine a scene's Story Event, answer these four Socratic questions:

1. The Action Story Component: What are the characters literally doing—that is, what are their micro on-the-surface actions?

Dorothy and Toto leave with provisions and set out on the yellow brick road. They spend the night with a grateful Munchkin family and the next morning set off again. On the road they meet a Scarecrow who is interested in going with them to Oz to get some brains.

2. The Worldview Story Component: What is the essential tactic of the characters—that is, what above-the-surface macro behaviors are they employing that are linked to a universal human value?

Dorothy sets off on a long walk to the City of Emeralds.

3. The Heroic Journey 2.0 Component: What beyond-the-surface universal human values have changed for one or more characters in the scene? Which one of those value changes is most important and should be included in the Story Grid Spreadsheet?

Dorothy and Toto set out alone on the path, get assistance from a happy Munchkin family and take on a fellow traveler in search of help the next day.

When in doubt, the Story Grid rule of thumb is to highlight the value that best aligns with the progress of the global human value at stake in the story. *The Wonderful Wizard of Oz* is an Action Story, which

has a global value at stake of Life/Death. Throughout the Story Grid Spreadsheet, we'll track the ways life is threatened or enhanced scene by scene.

As Dorothy and Toto have allies now (the Munchkin family and the Scarecrow) their universal human value of being alone has shifted into the enhanced positive of finding an allied group.

Alone to Together

4. The Scene Event Synthesis: What Story Event sums up the scene's on-the-surface actions, essential above-the-surface worldview behavioral tactics, and beyond-the-surface value change? We will enter that event in the Story Grid Spreadsheet.

After setting off for the City of Emeralds, Dorothy and Toto find allies in a Munchkin family and the Scarecrow.

HOW THE SCENE ABIDES BY THE FIVE COMMANDMENTS OF STORYTELLING

Inciting Incident: Dorothy prepares to leave the Munchkin house.

Turning Point Progressive Complication: Dorothy frees the Scarecrow from his pole.

Crisis: Best bad choice. If she allows the Scarecrow to come with her, he may prove to be a liability. If she doesn't invite him to come, she and Toto will have to face the dangers of the territory alone.

Climax: Dorothy invites the Scarecrow to come with her and Toto.

Resolution: The Scarecrow comes and carries Dorothy's basket for her.

NOTES

- Notice how L. Frank Baum is describing the new

extraordinary world in fine detail. This world is very different from the ordinary world he established in the first chapter—the gray world of Kansas and the depressing cheerlessness of it. The land of the Munchkins is beautiful and rich in color and sound and sunshine.

- The establishment of the strange land and the time with Boq and his family, who further establish the strangeness of the surroundings, builds into the introduction of the next magical element. The Scarecrow can talk. The mention of sorcerers, witches, etc., early on allows for this moment to be accepted by the reader. We've been forewarned about the necessity to suspend our disbelief. From chapter 1 things are happening that are beyond normal everyday reality.

- Great ending setup to establish the Scarecrow's vulnerability. His gift is in not feeling physical pain with the exception of a match, which will destroy him. He lacks, in his estimation, "brains."

4

THE ROAD THROUGH THE FOREST

SCENE 4

After a few hours the road began to be rough, and the walking grew so difficult that the **Scarecrow** often stumbled over the yellow bricks, which were here very uneven. Sometimes, indeed, they were broken or missing altogether, leaving holes that **Toto** jumped across and **Dorothy** walked around. As for the Scarecrow, having no brains, he walked straight ahead, and so stepped into the holes and fell at full length on the hard bricks. It never hurt him, however, and Dorothy would pick him up and set him upon his feet again, while he joined her in laughing merrily at his own mishap.

The farms were not nearly so well cared for here as they were farther back. There were fewer houses and fewer fruit trees, and the farther they went the more dismal and lonesome the country became.

At noon they sat down by the roadside, near a little brook, and Dorothy opened her basket and got out some bread. She offered a piece to the Scarecrow, but he refused.

"I am never hungry," he said, "and it is a lucky thing I am not, for my mouth is only painted, and if I should cut a hole in it so I could eat, the straw I am stuffed with would come out, and that would spoil the shape of my head."

Dorothy saw at once that this was true, so she only nodded and went on eating her bread.

"Tell me something about yourself and the country you came from," said the Scarecrow, when she had finished her dinner. So she told him all about Kansas, and how gray everything was there, and how the cyclone had carried her to this queer Land of Oz.

The Scarecrow listened carefully, and said, "I cannot understand why you should wish to leave this beautiful country and go back to the dry, gray place you call Kansas."

"That is because you have no brains" answered the girl. **"No matter how dreary and gray our homes are, we people of flesh and blood would rather live there than in any other country, be it ever so beautiful. There is no place like home."**

The Scarecrow sighed.

"Of course I cannot understand it," he said. "If your heads were stuffed with straw, like mine, you would probably all live in the beautiful places, and then Kansas would have no people at all. It is fortunate for Kansas that you have brains."

"Won't you tell me a story, while we are resting?" asked the child.

The Scarecrow looked at her reproachfully, and answered:

"My life has been so short that I really know nothing whatever. **I was only made day before yesterday.** What happened in the world before that time is all unknown to me. Luckily, when **the farmer** made my head, one of the first things he did was to paint my ears, so that I heard what was going on. There was **another Munchkin** with him, and the first thing I heard was the farmer saying, 'How do you like those ears?'

"'They aren't straight,'" answered the other.

"'Never mind,'" said the farmer. "'They are ears just the same,'" which was true enough.

"'Now I'll make the eyes,'" said the farmer. So he painted my right eye, and as soon as it was finished I found myself looking at him and at everything around me with a great deal of curiosity, for this was my first glimpse of the world.

"'That's a rather pretty eye,'" remarked the Munchkin who was watching the farmer. "'Blue paint is just the color for eyes.'

"'I think I'll make the other a little bigger,'" said the farmer. And when the second eye was done I could see much better than before. Then he made my nose and my mouth. But I did not speak, because at that time I didn't know what a mouth was for. I had the fun of watching them make my body and my arms and legs; and when they fastened on my head, at last, I felt very proud, for I thought I was just as good a man as anyone.

"'This fellow will scare the crows fast enough,' said the farmer. 'He looks just like a man.'

"'Why, he is a man,' said the other, and I quite agreed with him. The farmer carried me under his arm to the cornfield, and set me up on a tall stick, where you found me. He and his friend soon after walked away and left me alone.

"I did not like to be deserted this way. So I tried to walk after them. But my feet would not touch the ground, and I was forced to stay on that pole. It was a lonely life to lead, for I had nothing to think of, having been made such a little while before. Many crows and other birds flew into the cornfield, but as soon as they saw me they flew away again, thinking I was a Munchkin; and this pleased me and made me feel that I was quite an important person. By and by an old crow flew near me, and after looking at me carefully he perched upon my shoulder and said:

"'I wonder if that farmer thought to fool me in this clumsy manner. Any crow of sense could see that you are only stuffed with straw.' Then he hopped down at my feet and ate all the corn he wanted. The other birds, seeing he was not harmed by me, came to eat the corn too, so in a short time there was a great flock of them about me.

"I felt sad at this, for it showed I was not such a good Scarecrow after all; but the old crow comforted me, saying, 'If you only had brains in your head you would be as good a man as any of them, and a better man than some of them. Brains are the only things worth having in this world, no matter whether one is a crow or a man.'

"After the crows had gone I thought this over, and decided I would try hard to get some brains. By good luck you came along and pulled me off the stake, and from what you say I am sure the Great Oz will give me brains as soon as we get to the Emerald City."

"I hope so," said Dorothy earnestly, "since you seem anxious to have them."

"Oh, yes; I am anxious," returned the Scarecrow. "It is such an uncomfortable feeling to know one is a fool."

"Well," said the girl, "let us go." And she handed the basket to the Scarecrow.

There were no fences at all by the roadside now, and the land was rough and untilled. **Toward evening** they came to a great forest, where the trees grew so big and close together that their branches met over the road of yellow brick. It was almost dark under the trees, for the branches shut out the daylight; but the travelers did not stop, and went on into the forest.

"If this road goes in, it must come out," said the Scarecrow, "and as the Emerald City is at the other end of the road, we must go wherever it leads us."

"Anyone would know that," said Dorothy.

"Certainly; that is why I know it," returned the Scarecrow. "If it required brains to figure it out, I never should have said it."

After an hour or so the light faded away, and they found themselves stumbling along in the darkness. Dorothy could not see at all, but Toto could, for some dogs see very well in the dark; and the Scarecrow declared he could see as well as by day. So she took hold of his arm and managed to get along fairly well.

"If you see any house, or any place where we can pass the night," she said, "you must tell me; for it is very uncomfortable walking in the dark."

Soon after the Scarecrow stopped.

"I see a little cottage at the right of us," he said, "built of logs and branches. Shall we go there?"

"Yes, indeed," answered the child. "I am all tired out."

So the Scarecrow led her through the trees until they reached the cottage, and Dorothy entered and found a bed of dried leaves in one corner. She lay down at once, and with Toto beside her soon fell into a sound sleep. The Scarecrow, who was never tired, stood up in another corner and waited patiently until morning came.

STORY EVENT

A Story Event is an active change of a universal human value for one or more characters as a result of conflict (one character's desires clash with another's, or an environmental shift changes the universal human value).

A Working Scene contains at least one Story Event. To determine a scene's Story Event, answer these four Socratic questions:

1. The Action Story Component: What are the characters literally doing—that is, what are their micro on-the-surface actions?

Dorothy, Toto and the Scarecrow continue their journey into the dark stretches of the yellow brick road. They stop for lunch and then continue on until dark where the Scarecrow finds an old cabin just off the road.

2. The Worldview Story Component: What is the essential tactic of the characters—that is, what above-the-surface macro behaviors are they employing that are linked to a universal human value?

Dorothy and Scarecrow get to know each other as they move through the forest. Dorothy puts the Scarecrow in his place when he questions her devotion to Kansas.

3. The Heroic Journey 2.0 Component: What beyond-the-surface universal human values have changed for one or more characters in the scene? Which one of those value changes is most important and should be included in the Story Grid Spreadsheet?

Dorothy and Scarecrow share their stories. Dorothy tells Scarecrow about how she longs to get back to Kansas and Scarecrow tells her of how he came to life and failed at his job scaring off crows. An old crow told him he'd succeed if he got some brains, and then he'd be just like "a man."

Dorothy and the Scarecrow move from "Strangers to Companions," and Dorothy shifts their dynamic by moving from "confrontation to put in one's place."

When in doubt, the Story Grid rule of thumb is to highlight the value that best aligns with the progress of the global human value at stake in the story. *The Wonderful Wizard of Oz* is an Action Story, which has a global value at stake of Life/Death. Throughout the Story Grid Spreadsheet, we'll track the ways life is threatened or enhanced scene by scene.

As Dorothy is seizing the alpha position in this relationship, she is taking on the responsibility of leadership, which in this instance will threaten her survival more than enhance her survival.

Confrontation to Put in One's Place

4. The Scene Event Synthesis: What Story Event sums up the scene's on-the-surface actions, essential above-the-surface worldview behavioral tactics, and beyond-the-surface value change? We will enter that event in the Story Grid Spreadsheet.

Dorothy and the Scarecrow spend the day traveling together, getting to know each other, and establishing a power hierarchy between them.

HOW THE SCENE ABIDES BY THE FIVE COMMANDMENTS OF STORYTELLING

Inciting Incident: Lunchtime requires Dorothy to take a break and courtesy requires her to engage Scarecrow in conversation.

Turning Point Progressive Complication: Scarecrow confronts Dorothy about why she would want to return to a place that's gray like Kansas.

Crisis: Best bad choice. If Dorothy really thinks about what the

Scarecrow brought to her attention, she'd have to really consider the reality of Kansas as opposed to her fantasy about Kansas. Or she can blow off the Scarecrow's question by telling him he wouldn't understand because he is not flesh and blood and has no brains.

Climax: Dorothy tells the Scarecrow he wouldn't understand.

Resolution: The Scarecrow accepts Dorothy's explanation and resolves to prove himself to her by standing guard while she sleeps in a cabin he's found in the darkness of the forest.

5

THE RESCUE OF THE TIN WOODMAN

SCENE 5

When **Dorothy** awoke the sun was shining through the trees and **Toto** had long been out chasing birds around him and squirrels. She sat up and looked around her. There was the **Scarecrow**, still standing patiently in his corner, waiting for her.

"We must go and search for water," she said to him.

"Why do you want water?" he asked.

"To wash my face clean after the dust of the road, and to drink, so the dry bread will not stick in my throat."

"It must be inconvenient to be made of flesh," said the Scarecrow thoughtfully, "for you must sleep, and eat and drink. However, you have brains, and it is worth a lot of bother to be able to think properly."

They left the cottage and walked through the trees until they found a little spring of clear water, where Dorothy drank and bathed and ate her breakfast. She saw there was not much bread left in the basket, and the girl was thankful the Scarecrow did not have to eat anything, for there was scarcely enough for herself and Toto for the day.

When she had finished her meal, and was about to go back to the road of yellow brick, she was startled to hear a deep groan near by.

"What was that?" she asked timidly.

"I cannot imagine," replied the Scarecrow; "but we can go and see."

Just then another groan reached their ears, and the sound seemed to come from behind them. They turned and walked through the forest a few steps, when Dorothy discovered something shining in a ray of sunshine that fell between the trees. She ran to the place and then stopped short, with a little cry of surprise.

One of the big trees had been partly chopped through, and standing beside it, with an uplifted axe in his hands, was **a man made entirely of tin**. His head and arms and legs were jointed upon his body, but he stood perfectly motionless, as if he could not stir at all.

Dorothy looked at him in amazement, and so did the Scarecrow, while Toto barked sharply and made a snap at the tin legs, which hurt his teeth.

"Did you groan?" asked Dorothy.

"Yes," answered the tin man, "I did. I've been groaning for more than a year, and no one has ever heard me before or come to help me."

"What can I do for you?" she inquired softly, for she was moved by the sad voice in which the man spoke.

"Get an oil-can and oil my joints," he answered. "They are rusted so badly that I cannot move them at all; if I am well oiled I shall soon be all right again. You will find an oil-can on a shelf in my cottage."

Dorothy at once ran back to the cottage and found the oil-can, and then she returned and asked anxiously, "Where are your joints?"

"Oil my neck, first," replied the Tin Woodman. So she oiled it, and as it was quite badly rusted the Scarecrow took hold of the tin head and moved it gently from side to side until it worked freely, and then the man could turn it himself.

"Now oil the joints in my arms," he said. And Dorothy oiled them and the Scarecrow bent them carefully until they were quite free from rust and as good as new.

The Tin Woodman gave a sigh of satisfaction and lowered his axe, which he leaned against the tree.

"This is a great comfort," he said. "I have been holding that axe in the air ever since I rusted, and I'm glad to be able to put it down at last. Now, if you will oil the joints of my legs, I shall be all right once more."

So they oiled his legs until he could move them freely; and he thanked them again and again for his release, for he seemed a very polite creature, and very grateful.

"I might have stood there always if you had not come along," he said; "so you have certainly saved my life. How did you happen to be here?"

"We are on our way to the Emerald City to see **the Great Oz**," she answered, "and we stopped at your cottage to pass the night."

"Why do you wish to see Oz?" he asked.

"I want him to send me back to Kansas, and the Scarecrow wants him to put a few brains into his head," she replied.

The Tin Woodman appeared to think deeply for a moment. Then he said:

"Do you suppose Oz could give me a heart?"

"Why, I guess so," Dorothy answered. "It would be as easy as to give the Scarecrow brains."

"True," the Tin Woodman returned. "So, if you will allow me to join your party, I will also go to the Emerald City and ask Oz to help me."

"Come along," said the Scarecrow heartily, and Dorothy added that she would be pleased to have his company. So the Tin Woodman shouldered his axe and they all passed through the forest until they came to the road that was paved with yellow brick.

The Tin Woodman had asked Dorothy to put the oil-can in her basket. "For," he said, "if I should get caught in the rain, and rust again, I would need the oil-can badly."

It was a bit of good luck to have their new comrade join the party, for soon after they had begun their journey again they came to a place where the trees and branches grew so thick over the road that the travelers could not pass. But the Tin Woodman set to work with his axe and chopped so well that soon he cleared a passage for the entire party.

Dorothy was thinking so earnestly as they walked along that **she did not notice when the Scarecrow stumbled into a hole and rolled over to the side of the road. Indeed he was obliged to call to her to help him up again.**

"Why didn't you walk around the hole?" asked the Tin Woodman.

"I don't know enough," replied the Scarecrow cheerfully. "My head is stuffed with straw, you know, and that is why I am going to Oz to ask him for some brains."

"Oh, I see," said the Tin Woodman. "But, after all, brains are not the best things in the world."

"Have you any?" inquired the Scarecrow.

"No, my head is quite empty," answered the Woodman. "But once I had brains, and a heart also; so, having tried them both, I should much rather have a heart."

"And why is that?" asked the Scarecrow.

"I will tell you my story, and then you will know."

So, while they were walking through the forest, the Tin Woodman told the following story:

"I was born the son of **a woodman** who chopped down trees in the forest and sold the wood for a living. When I grew up, I too became a woodchopper, and after my father died I took care of **my old mother** as long as she lived. Then I made up my mind that instead of living alone I would marry, so that I might not become lonely.

"There was **one of the Munchkin girls** who was so beautiful that I soon grew to love her with all my heart. She, on her part, promised to marry me as soon as I could earn enough money to build a better house for her; so I set to work harder than ever. But the girl lived with **an old woman** who did not want her to marry anyone, for she was so lazy she wished the girl to remain with her and do the cooking and the housework. So the old woman went to **the Wicked Witch of the East**, and promised her two sheep and a cow if she would prevent the marriage. Thereupon the Wicked Witch enchanted my axe, and when I was chopping away at my best one day, for I was anxious to get the new house and my wife as soon as possible, the axe slipped all at once and cut off my left leg.

"This at first seemed a great misfortune, for I knew a one-legged man could not do very well as a wood-chopper. So I went to **a tinsmith** and had him make me a new leg out of tin. The leg worked very well, once I was used to it. But my action angered the Wicked Witch of the East, for she had promised the old woman I should not marry the pretty Munchkin girl. When I began chopping again, my axe slipped and cut off my right leg. Again I went to the tinsmith, and again he made me a leg out of tin. After this the enchanted axe cut off my arms, one after the other; but, nothing daunted, I had them replaced with tin ones. The Wicked Witch then made the axe slip and cut off my head, and at first I thought that was the end of me. But the tinsmith happened to come along, and he made me a new head out of tin.

"I thought I had beaten the Wicked Witch then, and I worked harder than ever; but I little knew how cruel my enemy could be. She thought of a new way to kill my love for the beautiful Munchkin maiden, and made my axe slip again, so that it cut right through my body, splitting me into two halves. Once more the tinsmith came to my help and made me a body of tin, fastening my tin arms and legs and head to it, by means of joints, so that I could move around as well as ever. But, alas! I had now no heart, so that I lost all my love for the Munchkin girl, and did not care whether I married her or not. I suppose she is still living with the old woman, waiting for me to come after her.

"My body shone so brightly in the sun that I felt very proud of it and it did not matter now if my axe slipped, for it could not cut me. There was only one danger—that my joints would rust; but I kept an oil-can in my cottage and took care to oil myself whenever I needed it. However, there came a day when I forgot to do this, and, being caught in a rainstorm, before I thought of the danger my joints had rusted, and I was left to stand in the woods until you came to help me. It was a terrible thing to undergo, but during the year I stood there I had time to think that the greatest loss I had known was the loss of my heart. While I was in love I was the happiest man on earth; but no one can love who has not a heart, and so I am resolved to ask Oz to give me one. If he does, I will go back to the Munchkin maiden and marry her."

Both Dorothy and the Scarecrow had been greatly interested in the story of the Tin Woodman, and now they knew why he was so anxious to get a new heart.

"All the same," said the Scarecrow, "I shall ask for brains instead of a heart; for a fool would not know what to do with a heart if he had one."

"I shall take the heart," returned the Tin Woodman; "for brains do not make one happy, and happiness is the best thing in the world."

Dorothy did not say anything, for she was puzzled to know which of her two friends was right, and she decided if she could only get back to Kansas and Aunt Em, it did not matter so much whether the Woodman had no brains and the Scarecrow no heart, or each got what he wanted.

What worried her most was that the bread was nearly gone, and another meal for herself and Toto would empty the basket. To be sure, neither the Woodman nor the Scarecrow ever ate anything, but she was not made of tin nor straw, and could not live unless she was fed.

• ANALYZING THE SCENE •

STORY EVENT

A Story Event is an active change of a universal human value for one or more characters as a result of conflict (one character's desires clash with another's, or an environmental shift changes the universal human value).

A Working Scene contains at least one Story Event. To determine a scene's Story Event, answer these four Socratic questions:

1. The Action Story Component: What are the characters literally doing—that is, what are their micro on-the-surface actions?

Dorothy, Toto and the Scarecrow wake the next morning, have breakfast, discover a rusted tin man, and proceed on their journey with another member of the party in search of a heart.

2. The Worldview Story Component: What is the essential tactic of the characters—that is, what above-the-surface macro behaviors are they employing that are linked to a universal human value?

Dorothy and the Scarecrow rescue a rusted Tin Woodman.

3. The Heroic Journey 2.0 Component: What beyond-the-surface universal human values have changed for one or more characters in the scene? Which one of those value changes is most important and should be included in the Story Grid Spreadsheet?

After the crew sets off on the yellow brick road, they reach an impasse where the trees have covered the brick. The tin man cuts the branches away so they can continue.

When in doubt, the Story Grid rule of thumb is to highlight the value that best aligns with the progress of the global human value at stake in the story. *The Wonderful Wizard of Oz* is an Action Story, which has a global value at stake of Life/Death. Throughout the Story Grid

Spreadsheet, we'll track the ways life is threatened or enhanced scene by scene.

Stopped to Started

4. The Scene Event Synthesis: What Story Event sums up the scene's on-the-surface actions, essential above-the-surface worldview behavioral tactics, and beyond-the-surface value change? We will enter that event in the Story Grid Spreadsheet.

Dorothy and the Scarecrow rescue a rusted Tin Woodman who joins their mission and cuts a pathway forward.

HOW THE SCENE ABIDES BY THE FIVE COMMANDMENTS OF STORYTELLING

Inciting Incident: A voice calls out from the wilderness.

Turning Point Progressive Complication: The pathway is choked with vegetation.

Crisis: Irreconcilable Goods: If the Tin Woodman cuts through the pathway, he'll be more susceptible to freezing up again as the oil will be worn away. If he doesn't, they won't be able to make it to the Emerald City.

Climax: The Tin Woodman cuts a pathway.

Resolution: The group moves on.

6

THE COWARDLY LION

SCENE 6

All this time **Dorothy** and **her companions** had been walking through the thick woods. The road was still paved with yellow brick, but these were much covered by dried branches and dead leaves from the trees, and the walking was not at all good.

There were few birds in this part of the forest, for birds love the open country where there is plenty of sunshine. But now and then there came a deep growl from some wild animal hidden among the trees. These sounds made the little girl's heart beat fast, for she did not know what made them; but **Toto** knew, and he walked close to Dorothy's side, and did not even bark in return.

"How long will it be," the child asked of the **Tin Woodman**, "before we are out of the forest?"

"I cannot tell," was the answer, "for I have never been to **the Emerald City**. But **my father** went there once, when I was a boy, and he said it was **a long journey through a dangerous country**, although nearer to the city where **Oz** dwells the country is beautiful. But I am not afraid so long as I have my oil-can, and nothing can hurt the **Scarecrow**, while you bear upon your forehead **the mark of the Good Witch's kiss**, and that will protect you from harm."

"But Toto!" said the girl anxiously. "What will protect him?"

"We must protect him ourselves if he is in danger," replied the Tin Woodman.

Just as he spoke there came from the forest a terrible roar, and the next moment **a great Lion** bounded into the road. With one blow of his paw he sent the **Scarecrow** spinning over and over to the edge of the road, and then he struck at the Tin Woodman with his sharp claws. But, to the Lion's surprise, he could make no impression on the tin, although the Woodman fell over in the road and lay still.

Little Toto, now that he had an enemy to face, ran barking toward the Lion, and the great beast had opened his mouth to bite the dog, when Dorothy, fearing Toto would be killed, and heedless of danger, rushed forward and slapped the Lion upon his nose as hard as she could, while she cried out:

"Don't you dare to bite Toto! You ought to be ashamed of yourself, a big beast like you, to bite a poor little dog!"

"I didn't bite him," said the Lion, as he rubbed his nose with his paw where Dorothy had hit it.

"No, but you tried to," she retorted. "You are nothing but a big coward."

"I know it," said the Lion, hanging his head in shame. "I've always known it. But how can I help it?"

"I don't know, I'm sure. To think of your striking a stuffed man, like the poor Scarecrow!"

"Is he stuffed?" asked the Lion in surprise, as he watched her pick up the Scarecrow and set him upon his feet, while she patted him into shape again.

"Of course he's stuffed," replied Dorothy, who was still angry.

"That's why he went over so easily," remarked the Lion. "It astonished me to see him whirl around so. Is the other one stuffed also?"

"No," said Dorothy, "he's made of tin." And she helped the Woodman up again.

"That's why he nearly blunted my claws," said the Lion. "When they scratched against the tin it made a cold shiver run down my back. What is that little animal you are so tender of?"

"He is my dog, Toto," answered Dorothy.

"Is he made of tin, or stuffed?" asked the Lion.

"Neither. He's a—a—a meat dog," said the girl.

"Oh! He's a curious animal and seems remarkably small, now that I look at him. No one would think of biting such a little thing, except a coward like me," continued the Lion sadly.

"What makes you a coward?" asked Dorothy, looking at the great beast in wonder, for he was as big as a small horse.

"It's a mystery," replied the Lion. "I suppose I was born that way. All the other animals in the forest naturally expect me to be brave, for the Lion is everywhere thought to be the King of Beasts. I learned that if I roared very loudly every living thing was frightened and got out of my way. Whenever I've met **a man** I've been awfully scared; but I just roared at him, and he has always run away as fast as he could go. If the elephants and the tigers and the bears had ever tried to fight me, I should have run myself—I'm such a coward; but just as soon as they hear me roar they all try to get away from me, and of course I let them go."

"But that isn't right. The King of Beasts shouldn't be a coward," said the Scarecrow.

"I know it," returned the Lion, wiping a tear from his eye with the tip of his tail. "It is my great sorrow, and makes my life very unhappy. But whenever there is danger, my heart begins to beat fast."

"Perhaps you have heart disease," said the Tin Woodman.

"It may be," said the Lion.

"If you have," continued the Tin Woodman, "you ought to be glad, for it proves you have a heart. For my part, I have no heart; so I cannot have heart disease."

"Perhaps," said the Lion thoughtfully, "if I had no heart I should not be a coward."

"Have you brains?" asked the Scarecrow.

"I suppose so. I've never looked to see," replied the Lion.

"I am going to the Great Oz to ask him to give me some," remarked the Scarecrow, "for my head is stuffed with straw."

"And I am going to ask him to give me a heart," said the Woodman.

"And I am going to ask him to send Toto and me back to Kansas," added Dorothy.

"Do you think Oz could give me courage?" asked the Cowardly Lion.

"Just as easily as he could give me brains," said the Scarecrow.

"Or give me a heart," said the Tin Woodman.

"Or send me back to Kansas," said Dorothy.

"Then, if you don't mind, I'll go with you," said the Lion, "for my life is simply unbearable without a bit of courage."

"You will be very welcome," answered Dorothy, "for you will help to keep away the other wild beasts. It seems to me they must be more cowardly than you are if they allow you to scare them so easily."

"They really are," said the Lion, "but that doesn't make me any braver, and as long as I know myself to be a coward I shall be unhappy."

So once more the little company set off upon the journey, the Lion walking with stately strides at Dorothy's side. Toto did not approve of this new comrade at first, for he could not forget how nearly he had been crushed between the Lion's great jaws. But after a time he became more at ease, and presently Toto and the Cowardly Lion had grown to be good friends.

During the rest of that day there was no other adventure to mar the peace of their journey. Once, indeed, the Tin Woodman stepped upon a beetle that was crawling along the road, and killed the poor little thing. This made the **Tin Woodman very unhappy, for he was always careful not to hurt any living creature; and as he walked along he wept several tears of sorrow and regret.** These tears ran slowly down his face and over the hinges of his jaw, and there they rusted. When Dorothy presently asked him a question the Tin Woodman could not open his mouth, for his jaws were tightly rusted together. He became greatly frightened at this and made many motions to Dorothy to relieve him, but she could not understand. The Lion was also puzzled to know what was wrong. **But the Scarecrow seized the oil-can from Dorothy's basket and oiled the Woodman's jaws, so that after a few moments he could talk as well as before.**

"This will serve me a lesson," said he, "to look where I step. For if I should kill another bug or beetle I should surely cry again, and crying rusts my jaws so that I cannot speak."

Thereafter he walked very carefully, with his eyes on the road, and when he saw a tiny ant toiling by he would step over it, so as not to harm it. The Tin Woodman knew very well he had no heart, and therefore he took great care never to be cruel or unkind to anything.

"You people with hearts," he said, "have something to guide you, and need never do wrong; but I have no heart, and so I must be very careful. When Oz gives me a heart of course I needn't mind so much."

• ANALYZING THE SCENE •

STORY EVENT

A Story Event is an active change of a universal human value for one or more characters as a result of conflict (one character's desires clash with another's, or an environmental shift changes the universal human value).

A Working Scene contains at least one Story Event. To determine a scene's Story Event, answer these four Socratic questions:

1. The Action Story Component: What are the characters literally doing—that is, what are their micro on-the-surface actions?

Dorothy, Toto, the Scarecrow, and the Tin Woodman confront a lion on their way down the yellow brick road's darkest section.

2. The Worldview Story Component: What is the essential tactic of the characters—that is, what above-the-surface macro behaviors are they employing that are linked to a universal human value?

Dorothy defends Toto after the cowardly lion tosses aside the Scarecrow and the Tin Woodman.

3. The Heroic Journey 2.0 Component: What beyond-the-surface universal human values have changed for one or more characters in the scene? Which one of those value changes is most important and should be included in the Story Grid Spreadsheet?

All four allied characters are threatened until Dorothy confronts the lion, who quickly confesses to being a coward.

When in doubt, the Story Grid rule of thumb is to highlight the value that best aligns with the progress of the global human value at stake in the story. *The Wonderful Wizard of Oz* is an Action Story, which has a global value at stake of Life/Death. Throughout the Story Grid

Spreadsheet, we'll track the ways life is threatened or enhanced scene by scene.

Unsafe to Safe

4. The Scene Event Synthesis: What Story Event sums up the scene's on-the-surface actions, essential above-the-surface worldview behavioral tactics, and beyond-the-surface value change? We will enter that event in the Story Grid Spreadsheet.

Dorothy defends Toto from an attack by a lion.

HOW THE SCENE ABIDES BY THE FIVE COMMANDMENTS OF STORYTELLING

Inciting Incident: A lion jumps onto the yellow brick road.

Turning Point Progressive Complication: Dorothy smacks the lion on the nose.

Crisis: Best bad choice. If the lion attacks, he may get hurt even worse. If he doesn't attack, he'll be considered a coward.

Climax: The lion backs off.

Resolution: The lion confesses he's a coward and then joins the group to see if he can get the Wizard of Oz to grant him courage.

7

THE JOURNEY TO THE GREAT OZ

SCENE 7

They were obliged to camp out that night under a large tree in the forest, for there were no houses near. The tree made a good, thick covering to protect them from the dew, and **the Tin Woodman** chopped a great pile of wood with his axe and **Dorothy** built a splendid fire that warmed her and made her feel less lonely. She and **Toto** ate **the last of their bread**, and now she did not know what they would do for breakfast.

"If you wish," said **the Lion**, "I will go into the forest and kill a deer for you. You can roast it by the fire, since your tastes are so peculiar that you prefer cooked food, and then you will have a very good breakfast."

"Don't! Please don't," begged the Tin Woodman. "I should certainly weep if you killed a poor deer, and then my jaws would rust again."

But the Lion went away into the forest and found his own supper, and no one ever knew what it was, for he didn't mention it. And **the Scarecrow** found a tree full of nuts and filled Dorothy's basket with them, so that she would not be hungry for a long time. She thought this was very kind and thoughtful of the Scarecrow, but she laughed heartily at the awkward way in which the poor creature picked up the nuts. His padded hands were so clumsy and the nuts were so small that he dropped almost as many as he put in the basket. But the Scarecrow did not mind how long it took him to fill the basket, for it enabled him to keep away from the fire, as he feared a spark might get into his straw and burn him up. So he kept a good distance away from the flames, and only came near to cover Dorothy with dry leaves when she lay down to sleep. These kept her very snug and warm, and she slept soundly until morning.

When it was daylight, the girl bathed her face in a little rippling brook, and soon after they all started toward the Emerald City.

This was to be an eventful day for the travelers. They had hardly been walking an hour when they saw before them a great ditch that crossed the road and divided the forest as far as they could see on either side. It was a very wide ditch, and when they crept up to the edge and looked into it they could see it was also very deep, and there were many big, jagged rocks at the bottom. The sides were so steep that none of them could climb down, and for a moment it seemed that their journey must end.

"What shall we do?" asked Dorothy despairingly.

"I haven't the faintest idea," said the Tin Woodman, and the Lion shook his shaggy mane and looked thoughtful.

But the Scarecrow said, "We cannot fly, that is certain. Neither can we climb down into this great ditch. Therefore, if we cannot jump over it, we must stop where we are."

"I think I could jump over it," said the Cowardly Lion, after measuring the distance carefully in his mind.

"Then we are all right," answered the Scarecrow, "for you can carry us all over on your back, one at a time."

"Well, I'll try it," said the Lion. "Who will go first?"

"I will," declared the Scarecrow, "for, if you found that you could not jump over the gulf, Dorothy would be killed, or the Tin Woodman badly dented on the rocks below. But if I am on your back it will not matter so much, for the fall would not hurt me at all."

"I am terribly afraid of falling, myself," said the Cowardly Lion, "but I suppose there is nothing to do but try it. So get on my back and we will make the attempt."

The Scarecrow sat upon the Lion's back, and the big beast walked to the edge of the gulf and crouched down.

"Why don't you run and jump?" asked the Scarecrow.

"Because that isn't the way we Lions do these things," he replied. Then giving a great spring, he shot through the air and landed safely on the other side. They were all greatly pleased to see how easily he did it, and after the Scarecrow had got down from his back the Lion sprang across the ditch again.

Dorothy thought she would go next; so she took **Toto** in her arms and climbed on the Lion's back, holding tightly to his mane with one hand. The next moment it seemed as if she were flying through the air; and then, before she had time to think about it, she was safe on the other side. The Lion went back a third time and got the Tin Woodman, and then they all sat down for a few moments to give the beast a chance to rest, for his great leaps had made his breath short, and he panted like a big dog that has been running too long.

They found the forest very thick on this side, and it looked dark and gloomy. After the Lion had rested they started along the road of yellow brick, silently wondering, each in his own mind, if ever they would come to the end of the woods and reach the bright sunshine again. To add to their discomfort, they soon heard strange noises in the depths of the forest, and the Lion whispered to them that it was in this part of the country that **the Kalidahs** lived.

"What are the Kalidahs?" asked the girl.

"They are monstrous beasts with bodies like bears and heads like tigers," replied the Lion, "and with claws so long and sharp that they could tear me in two as easily as I could kill Toto. I'm terribly afraid of the Kalidahs."

"I'm not surprised that you are," returned Dorothy. "They must be dreadful beasts."

The Lion was about to reply when suddenly they came to another gulf across the road. But this one was so broad and deep that the Lion knew at once he could not leap across it.

So they sat down to consider what they should do, and after serious thought the Scarecrow said:

"Here is a great tree, standing close to the ditch. If the Tin

Woodman can chop it down, so that it will fall to the other side, we can walk across it easily."

"That is a first-rate idea," said the Lion. "One would almost suspect you had brains in your head, instead of straw."

The Woodman set to work at once, and so sharp was his axe that the tree was soon chopped nearly through. Then the Lion put his strong front legs against the tree and pushed with all his might, and slowly the big tree tipped and fell with a crash across the ditch, with its top branches on the other side.

They had just started to cross this queer bridge when a sharp growl made them all look up, and to their horror they saw running toward them two great beasts with bodies like bears and heads like tigers.

"They are the Kalidahs!" said the Cowardly Lion, beginning to tremble.

"Quick!" cried the Scarecrow. "Let us cross over."

So Dorothy went first, holding Toto in her arms, the Tin Woodman followed, and the Scarecrow came next. The Lion, although he was certainly afraid, turned to face the Kalidahs, and then he gave so loud and terrible a roar that Dorothy screamed and the Scarecrow fell over backward, while even the fierce beasts stopped short and looked at him in surprise.

But, seeing they were bigger than the Lion, and remembering that there were two of them and only one of him, the Kalidahs again rushed forward, and the Lion crossed over the tree and turned to see what they would do next. Without stopping an instant the fierce beasts also began to cross the tree. And the Lion said to Dorothy:

"We are lost, for they will surely tear us to pieces with their sharp claws. But stand close behind me, and I will fight them as long as I am alive."

"Wait a minute!" called the Scarecrow. He had been thinking what was best to be done, and now he asked the Woodman to chop away the end of the tree that rested on their side of the ditch. The Tin Woodman began to use his axe at once, and, just as the two Kalidahs were nearly across, the tree fell with a crash into the gulf, carrying the ugly, snarling brutes with it, and both were dashed to pieces on the sharp rocks at the bottom.

"Well," said the Cowardly Lion, drawing a long breath of relief, "I see we are going to live a little while longer, and I am glad of it, for it must be a very uncomfortable thing not to be alive. Those creatures frightened me so badly that my heart is beating yet."

"Ah," said the Tin Woodman sadly, "I wish I had a heart to beat."

This adventure made the travelers more anxious than ever to get out of the forest, and they walked so fast that Dorothy became tired, and had to ride on the Lion's back. To their great joy the trees became thinner the farther they advanced, **and in the afternoon** they suddenly came upon a broad river, flowing swiftly just before them. On the other side of the water they could see the road of yellow brick running through a beautiful country, with green meadows dotted with bright flowers and all the road bordered with **trees hanging full of delicious fruits**. They were greatly pleased to see this delightful country before them.

"How shall we cross the river?" asked Dorothy.

"That is easily done," replied the Scarecrow. "The Tin Woodman must build us a raft, so we can float to the other side."

So the Woodman took his axe and began to chop down small trees to make a raft, and while he was busy at this the Scarecrow found on the riverbank a tree full of fine fruit. This pleased Dorothy, who had eaten nothing but nuts all day, and she made a hearty meal of the ripe fruit.

But it takes time to make a raft, even when one is as industrious and untiring as the Tin Woodman, and **when night came** the work was not done. So they found a cozy place under the trees where they slept well until the morning; and Dorothy dreamed of the Emerald City, and of the **good Wizard Oz**, who would soon send her back to her own home again.

STORY EVENT

A Story Event is an active change of a universal human value for one or more characters as a result of conflict (one character's desires clash with another's, or an environmental shift changes the universal human value).

A Working Scene contains at least one Story Event. To determine a scene's Story Event, answer these four Socratic questions:

1. The Action Story Component: What are the characters literally doing—that is, what are their micro on-the-surface actions?

Dorothy, Toto, the Scarecrow, the Tin Woodman, and the Lion solve a series of challenges along the yellow brick road that threaten to stop their progress.

2. The Worldview Story Component: What is the essential tactic of the characters—that is, what above-the-surface macro behaviors are they employing that are linked to a universal human value?

The crew is relying upon one another as members of a team. The individual with the best skill set to solve the problem takes the leadership role and the others take supporting roles.

3. The Heroic Journey 2.0 Component: What beyond-the-surface universal human values have changed for one or more characters in the scene? Which one of those value changes is most important and should be included in the Story Grid Spreadsheet?

All of the challenges the crew faces are life-threatening and they successfully avoid death on every occasion.

When in doubt, the Story Grid rule of thumb is to highlight the value that best aligns with the progress of the global human value at stake in the story. *The Wonderful Wizard of Oz* is an Action Story, which

has a global value at stake of Life/Death. Throughout the Story Grid Spreadsheet, we'll track the ways life is threatened or enhanced scene by scene.

Mortally Threatened to Skillfully Alive

4. The Scene Event Synthesis: What Story Event sums up the scene's on-the-surface actions, essential above-the-surface worldview behavioral tactics, and beyond-the-surface value change? We will enter that event in the Story Grid Spreadsheet.

The Scarecrow displays keen insight, and the lion displays considerable courage as the group navigates closer to the Emerald City.

HOW THE SCENE ABIDES BY THE FIVE COMMANDMENTS OF STORYTELLING

Inciting Incident: Dorothy has run out of food.

Turning Point Progressive Complication: There is a gap in the road. The Kalidahs attack. The river separates them from the yellow brick road.

Crisis: Best bad choice. Should the lion risk his life to jump over the gap? Or should he save himself and leave his companions stranded?

Climax: The Lion jumps over the chasm with each of his friends on his back. And the rest of the hurdles are faced with similar aplomb.

Resolution: Together the group is able to keep moving forward.

8

THE DEADLY POPPY FIELD

SCENE 8

Our little party of travelers awakened the next morning refreshed and full of hope, and **Dorothy** breakfasted like a princess off peaches and plums from the trees beside the river. Behind them was the dark forest they had passed safely through, although they had suffered many discouragements; but before them was a lovely, sunny country that seemed to beckon them on to the Emerald City.

To be sure, the broad river now cut them off from this beautiful land. But the raft was nearly done, and after **the Tin Woodman** had cut a few more logs and fastened them together with wooden pins, they were ready to start. Dorothy sat down in the middle of the raft and held **Toto** in her arms. When the **Cowardly Lion** stepped upon the raft it tipped badly, for he was big and heavy; but **the Scarecrow** and the Tin Woodman stood upon the other end to steady it, and they had long poles in their hands to push the raft through the water.

They got along quite well at first, but when they reached the middle of the river the swift current swept the raft downstream, farther and farther away from the road of yellow brick. And the water grew so deep that the long poles would not touch the bottom.

"This is bad," said the Tin Woodman, "for if we cannot get to the land we shall be carried into the country of **the Wicked Witch of the West**, and she will enchant us and make us her slaves."

"And then I should get no brains," said the Scarecrow.

"And I should get no courage," said the Cowardly Lion.

"And I should get no heart," said the Tin Woodman.

"And I should never get back to Kansas," said Dorothy.

"We must certainly get to the Emerald City if we can," the Scarecrow continued, and he pushed so hard on his long pole that it stuck fast in the mud at the bottom of the river. Then, before he could pull it out again—or let go—the raft was swept away, and the poor Scarecrow was left clinging to the pole in the middle of the river.

"Good-bye!" he called after them, and they were very sorry to leave him. Indeed, the Tin Woodman began to cry, but fortunately remembered that he might rust, and so dried his tears on Dorothy's apron.

Of course this was a bad thing for the Scarecrow.

"I am now worse off than when I first met Dorothy," he thought. "Then, I was stuck on a pole in a cornfield, where I could make-believe scare the crows, at any rate. But surely there is no use for a Scarecrow stuck on a pole in the middle of a river. I am afraid I shall never have any brains, after all!"

Down the stream the raft floated, and the poor Scarecrow was left far behind. Then the Lion said:

"Something must be done to save us. I think I can swim to the shore and pull the raft after me, if you will only hold fast to the tip of my tail."

So he sprang into the water, and the Tin Woodman caught fast hold of his tail. Then the Lion began to swim with all his might toward the shore. It was hard work, although he was so big; but by and by they were drawn out of the current, and then Dorothy took the Tin Woodman's long pole and helped push the raft to the land.

They were all tired out when they reached the shore at last and stepped off upon the pretty green grass, and they also knew that the stream had carried them a long way past the road of yellow brick that led to the Emerald City.

"What shall we do now?" asked the Tin Woodman, as the Lion lay down on the grass to let the sun dry him.

"We must get back to the road, in some way," said Dorothy.

"The best plan will be to walk along the riverbank until we come to the road again," remarked the Lion.

So, when they were rested, Dorothy picked up her basket and they started along the grassy bank, to the road from which the river had carried them. It was a lovely country, with plenty of flowers and fruit trees and sunshine to cheer them, and had they not felt so sorry for the poor Scarecrow, they could have been very happy.

They walked along as fast as they could, Dorothy only stopping once to pick a beautiful flower; and after a time the Tin Woodman cried out: "Look!"

Then they all looked at the river and saw the Scarecrow perched upon his pole in the middle of the water, looking very lonely and sad.

"What can we do to save him?" asked Dorothy.

The Lion and the Woodman both shook their heads, for they did not know. So they sat down upon the bank and gazed wistfully at the Scarecrow until **a Stork** flew by, who, upon seeing them, stopped to rest at the water's edge.

"Who are you and where are you going?" asked the Stork.

"I am Dorothy," answered the girl, "and these are my friends, the Tin Woodman and the Cowardly Lion; and we are going to the Emerald City."

"This isn't the road," said the Stork, as she twisted her long neck and looked sharply at the queer party.

"I know it," returned Dorothy, "but we have lost the Scarecrow, and are wondering how we shall get him again."

"Where is he?" asked the Stork.

"Over there in the river," answered the little girl.

"If he wasn't so big and heavy I would get him for you," remarked the Stork.

"He isn't heavy a bit," said Dorothy eagerly, "for he is stuffed with straw; and if you will bring him back to us, we shall thank you ever and ever so much."

"Well, I'll try," said the Stork, "but if I find he is too heavy to carry I shall have to drop him in the river again."

So the big bird flew into the air and over the water till she came to where the Scarecrow was perched upon his pole. Then the Stork with her great claws grabbed the Scarecrow by the arm and carried him up into the air and back to the bank, where Dorothy and the Lion and the Tin Woodman and Toto were sitting.

When the Scarecrow found himself among his friends again, he was so happy that he hugged them all, even the Lion and Toto; and as they walked along he sang "Tol-de-ri-de-oh!" at every step, he felt so gay.

"I was afraid I should have to stay in the river forever," he said, "but the kind Stork saved me, and if I ever get any brains I shall find the Stork again and do her some kindness in return."

"That's all right," said the Stork, who was flying along beside them. "I always like to help anyone in trouble. But I must go now, for **my babies** are waiting in the nest for me. I hope you will find the Emerald City and that **Oz** will help you."

"Thank you," replied Dorothy, and then the kind Stork flew into the air and was soon out of sight.

They walked along listening to the singing of the brightly colored birds and looking at the lovely flowers which now became so thick that the ground was carpeted with them. There were big yellow and white and blue and purple blossoms, besides great clusters of scarlet poppies, which were so brilliant in color they almost dazzled Dorothy's eyes.

"Aren't they beautiful?" the girl asked, as she breathed in the spicy scent of the bright flowers.

"I suppose so," answered the Scarecrow. "When I have brains, I shall probably like them better."

"If I only had a heart, I should love them," added the Tin Woodman.

"I always did like flowers," said the Lion. "They seem so helpless and frail. But there are none in the forest so bright as these."

They now came upon more and more of the big scarlet poppies, and fewer and fewer of the other flowers; and soon they found themselves in the midst of a great meadow of poppies. Now it is well known that when there are many of these flowers together their odor is so powerful that anyone who breathes it falls asleep, and if the sleeper is not carried away from the scent of the flowers, he sleeps on and on forever. But Dorothy did not know this, nor could she get away from the bright red flowers that were everywhere about; so presently her eyes grew heavy and she felt she must sit down to rest and to sleep.

But the Tin Woodman would not let her do this.

"We must hurry and get back to the road of yellow brick before dark," he said; and the Scarecrow agreed with him. So they kept walking until Dorothy could stand no longer. Her eyes closed in spite of herself and she forgot where she was and fell among the poppies, fast asleep.

"What shall we do?" asked the Tin Woodman.

"If we leave her here she will die," said the Lion. "The smell of the flowers is killing us all. I myself can scarcely keep my eyes open, and the dog is asleep already."

It was true; Toto had fallen down beside his little mistress. But the Scarecrow and the Tin Woodman, not being made of flesh, were not troubled by the scent of the flowers.

"Run fast," said the Scarecrow to the Lion, "and get out of this deadly flower bed as soon as you can. We will bring the little girl with us, but if you should fall asleep you are too big to be carried."

So the Lion aroused himself and bounded forward as fast as he could go. In a moment he was out of sight.

"Let us make a chair with our hands and carry her," said the Scarecrow. So they picked up Toto and put the dog in Dorothy's lap, and then they made a chair with their hands for the seat and their arms for the arms and carried the sleeping girl between them through the flowers.

On and on they walked, and it seemed that the great carpet of deadly flowers that surrounded them would never end. They followed the bend of the river, and at last came upon their friend the Lion, lying fast asleep among the poppies. The flowers had been too strong for the huge beast and he had given up at last, and fallen only a short distance from the end of the poppy bed, where the sweet grass spread in beautiful green fields before them.

"We can do nothing for him," said the Tin Woodman, sadly; "for he is much too heavy to lift. We must leave him here to sleep on forever, and perhaps he will dream that he has found courage at last."

"I'm sorry," said the Scarecrow. "The Lion was a very good comrade for one so cowardly. But let us go on."

They carried the sleeping girl to a pretty spot beside the river, far enough from the poppy field to prevent her breathing any more of the poison of the flowers, and here they laid her gently on the soft grass and waited for the fresh breeze to waken her.

• ANALYZING THE SCENE •

STORY EVENT

A Story Event is an active change of a universal human value for one or more characters as a result of conflict (one character's desires clash with another's, or an environmental shift changes the universal human value).

A Working Scene contains at least one Story Event. To determine a scene's Story Event, answer these four Socratic questions:

1. The Action Story Component: What are the characters literally doing—that is, what are their micro on-the-surface actions?

Dorothy, Toto, the Scarecrow, the Tin Woodman, and the Lion confront a raging river and a poppy field along the yellow brick road that threaten to stop their progress.

2. The Worldview Story Component: What is the essential tactic of the characters—that is, what above-the-surface macro behaviors are they employing that are linked to a universal human value?

Each member of the group is applying their highest cognitive capacities to solve their navigational problems under the constraints of holding the group together.

3. The Heroic Journey 2.0 Component: What beyond-the-surface universal human values have changed for one or more characters in the scene? Which one of those value changes is most important and should be included in the Story Grid Spreadsheet?

All of the players in the group face life and death circumstances and the scene ends with an unconscious Dorothy and Lion.

When in doubt, the Story Grid rule of thumb is to highlight the value that best aligns with the progress of the global human value at stake in the story. *The Wonderful Wizard of Oz* is an Action Story, which

has a global value at stake of Life/Death. Throughout the Story Grid Spreadsheet, we'll track the ways life is threatened or enhanced scene by scene.

Conscious to Unconscious

4. The Scene Event Synthesis: What Story Event sums up the scene's on-the-surface actions, essential above-the-surface worldview behavioral tactics, and beyond-the-surface value change? We will enter that event in the Story Grid Spreadsheet.

The band of companions face a raging river and a poppy field that anaesthetizes Dorothy and the Lion as they travel down the yellow brick road.

HOW THE SCENE ABIDES BY THE FIVE COMMANDMENTS OF STORYTELLING

Inciting Incident: The raft is ready to use.

Turning Point Progressive Complication: The Scarecrow sticks to the pole in the river. The Stork saves the Scarecrow. Dorothy and the Lion are drugged by the poppy field.

Crisis: Best bad choice. If they leave the Lion in the poppy field, he'll die. If they try and bring him out, they'll never succeed.

Climax: The Tin Woodman and Scarecrow get Dorothy and Toto out of the field but not the Lion.

Resolution: The Lion is fast asleep in the poppy field.

9

THE QUEEN OF THE FIELD MICE

SCENE 9

"We cannot be far from the road of yellow brick, now," remarked **the Scarecrow**, as he stood beside the **girl**, "for we have come nearly as far as the river carried us away."

The Tin Woodman was about to reply when he heard a low growl, and turning his head (which worked beautifully on hinges) he saw a strange beast come bounding over the grass toward them. It was, indeed, a great yellow **Wildcat,** and the Woodman thought it must be chasing something, for its ears were lying close to its head and its mouth was wide open, showing two rows of ugly teeth, while its red eyes glowed like balls of fire. As it came nearer the Tin Woodman saw that running before the beast was **a little gray field mouse**, and although he had no heart he knew it was wrong for the Wildcat to try to kill such a pretty, harmless creature.

So the Woodman raised his axe, and as the Wildcat ran by he gave it a quick blow that cut the beast's head clean off from its body, and it rolled over at his feet in two pieces.

The field mouse, now that it was freed from its enemy, stopped short; and coming slowly up to the Woodman it said, in a squeaky little voice:

"Oh, thank you! Thank you ever so much for saving my life."

"Don't speak of it, I beg of you," replied the Woodman. **"I have no heart, you know, so I am careful to help all those who may need a friend, even if it happens to be only a mouse."**

"Only a mouse!" cried the little animal, indignantly. "Why, I am a Queen—the Queen of all the Field Mice!"

"Oh, indeed," said the Woodman, making a bow.

"Therefore you have done a great deed, as well as a brave one, in saving my life," added the Queen.

At that moment **several mice** were seen running up as fast as their little legs could carry them, and when they saw their Queen they exclaimed:

"Oh, your Majesty, we thought you would be killed! How did you manage to escape the great Wildcat?" They all bowed so low to the little Queen that they almost stood upon their heads.

"This funny tin man," she answered, "killed the Wildcat and saved my life. So hereafter you must all serve him, and obey his slightest wish."

"We will!" cried all the mice, in a shrill chorus. And then they scampered in all directions, for **Toto** had awakened from his sleep, and seeing all these mice around him he gave one bark of delight and jumped right into the middle of the group. Toto had always loved to chase mice when he lived in Kansas, and he saw no harm in it.

But the Tin Woodman caught the dog in his arms and held him tight, while he called to the mice, "Come back! Come back! Toto shall not hurt you."

At this the Queen of the Mice stuck her head out from underneath a clump of grass and asked, in a timid voice, "Are you sure he will not bite us?"

"I will not let him," said the Woodman; "so do not be afraid."

One by one the mice came creeping back, and Toto did not bark again, although he tried to get out of the Woodman's arms, and would have bitten him had he not known very well he was made of tin. Finally one of the biggest mice spoke.

"Is there anything we can do," it asked, "to repay you for saving the life of our Queen?"

"Nothing that I know of," answered the Woodman; but the **Scarecrow, who had been trying to think, but could not because his head was stuffed with straw, said, quickly, "Oh, yes; you can save our friend, the Cowardly Lion, who is asleep in the poppy bed."**

"A Lion!" cried the little Queen. "Why, he would eat us all up."

"Oh, no," declared the Scarecrow; "this Lion is a coward."

"Really?" asked the Mouse.

"He says so himself," answered the Scarecrow, "and he would never hurt anyone who is our friend. If you will help us to save him I promise that he shall treat you all with kindness."

"Very well," said the Queen, "we trust you. But what shall we do?"

"Are there many of these mice which call you Queen and are willing to obey you?"

"Oh, yes; there are thousands," she replied.

"Then send for them all to come here as soon as possible, and let each one bring a long piece of string."

The Queen turned to the mice that attended her and told them to go at once and get all her people. As soon as they heard her orders they ran away in every direction as fast as possible.

"Now," said the Scarecrow to the Tin Woodman, "you must go to those trees by the riverside and make a truck that will carry the Lion."

So the Woodman went at once to the trees and began to work; and he soon made a truck out of the limbs of trees, from which he chopped away all the leaves and branches. He fastened it together with wooden pegs and made the four wheels out of short pieces of a big tree trunk. So fast and so well did he work that by the time the mice began to arrive the truck was all ready for them.

They came from all directions, and there were thousands of them: big mice and little mice and middle-sized mice; and each one brought a piece of string in his mouth. It was about this time that **Dorothy** woke from her long sleep and opened her eyes. She was greatly astonished to find herself lying upon the grass, with thousands of mice standing around and looking at her timidly. But the Scarecrow told her about everything, and turning to the dignified little Mouse, he said:

"Permit me to introduce to you her Majesty, the Queen."

Dorothy nodded gravely and the Queen made a curtsy, after which she became quite friendly with the little girl.

The Scarecrow and the Woodman now began to fasten the mice to the truck, using the strings they had brought. One end of a string was tied around the neck of each mouse and the other end to the truck. Of course the truck was a thousand times bigger than any of the mice who were to draw it; but when all the mice had been harnessed, they were able to pull it quite easily. Even the Scarecrow and the Tin Woodman could sit on it, and were drawn swiftly by their queer little horses to the place where the Lion lay asleep.

After a great deal of hard work, for the Lion was heavy, they managed to get him up on the truck. Then the Queen hurriedly gave her people the order to start, for she feared if the mice stayed among the poppies too long they also would fall asleep.

At first the little creatures, many though they were, could hardly stir the heavily loaded truck; but the Woodman and the Scarecrow both pushed from behind, and they got along better. Soon they rolled the Lion out of the poppy bed to the green fields, where he could breathe the sweet, fresh air again, instead of the poisonous scent of the flowers.

Dorothy came to meet them and thanked the little mice warmly for saving her companion from death. She had grown so fond of the big Lion she was glad he had been rescued.

Then the mice were unharnessed from the truck and scampered away through the grass to their homes. The Queen of the Mice was the last to leave.

"If ever you need us again," she said, "come out into the field and call, and we shall hear you and come to your assistance. Good-bye!"

"Good-bye!" they all answered, and away the Queen ran, while Dorothy held Toto tightly lest he should run after her and frighten her.

After this they sat down beside the Lion until he should awaken; and the Scarecrow brought Dorothy some fruit from a tree near by, which she ate for her dinner.

• ANALYZING THE SCENE •

STORY EVENT

A Story Event is an active change of a universal human value for one or more characters as a result of conflict (one character's desires clash with another's, or an environmental shift changes the universal human value).

A Working Scene contains at least one Story Event. To determine a scene's Story Event, answer these four Socratic questions:

1. The Action Story Component: What are the characters literally doing—that is, what are their micro on-the-surface actions?

The Tin Woodman saves the queen of the field mice from a wildcat and the Scarecrow figures out how to use the mice to get the Lion out of the poppy field.

2. The Worldview Story Component: What is the essential tactic of the characters—that is, what above-the-surface macro behaviors are they employing that are linked to a universal human value?

The Tin Woodman acts out his kindhearted worldview when he sees an injustice, and the Scarecrow uses his innate insight generative capacity to leverage the woodman's kindness.

3. The Heroic Journey 2.0 Component: What beyond-the-surface universal human values have changed for one or more characters in the scene? Which one of those value changes is most important and should be included in the Story Grid Spreadsheet?

Life and death stakes continue to drive the story as the Tin Woodman saves the life of the queen of the field mice, who returns the favor by saving the Lion's life.

When in doubt, the Story Grid rule of thumb is to highlight the value that best aligns with the progress of the global human value at stake in the story. *The Wonderful Wizard of Oz* is an Action Story, which has a global value at stake of Life/Death. Throughout the Story Grid Spreadsheet, we'll track the ways life is threatened or enhanced scene by scene.

Unconscious to Conscious

4. The Scene Event Synthesis: What Story Event sums up the scene's on-the-surface actions, essential above-the-surface worldview behavioral tactics, and beyond-the-surface value change? We will enter that event in the Story Grid Spreadsheet.

The Tin Woodman and the Scarecrow figure out how to save the Lion with the help of field mice.

HOW THE SCENE ABIDES BY THE FIVE COMMANDMENTS OF STORYTELLING

Inciting Incident: A wildcat chases a field mouse.

Turning Point Progressive Complication: The field mouse turns out to be the queen of all the mice.

Crisis: Irreconcilable Goods: If the mice save the Lion, he could kill them, but to not save the Lion is to not repay the life-giving gift of the Tin Woodman.

Climax: The queen of the field mice orders her subjects to help the Tin Woodman and Scarecrow.

Resolution: Together the group is able to move the Lion into safe fields.

10

THE GUARDIAN OF THE GATE

SCENE 10

It was some time before **the Cowardly Lion** awakened, for he had lain among the poppies a long while, breathing in their deadly fragrance; but when he did open his eyes and roll off the truck he was very glad to find himself still alive.

"I ran as fast as I could," he said, sitting down and yawning, "but the flowers were too strong for me. How did you get me out?"

Then they told him of **the field mice**, and how they had generously saved him from death; and the Cowardly Lion laughed, and said:

"I have always thought myself very big and terrible; yet such little things as flowers came near to killing me, and such small animals as mice have saved my life. How strange it all is! But, comrades, what shall we do now?"

"We must journey on until we find the road of yellow brick again," said **Dorothy**, "and then we can keep on to the Emerald City."

So, the Lion being fully refreshed, and feeling quite himself again, they all started upon the journey, greatly enjoying the walk through the soft, fresh grass; and it was not long before they reached the road of yellow brick and turned again toward the Emerald City where the **Great Oz** dwelt.

The road was smooth and well paved, now, and the country about was beautiful, so that the travelers rejoiced in leaving the forest far behind, and with it the many dangers they had met in its gloomy shades. Once more they could see fences built beside the road; but these were painted green, and when they came to a small house, in which a farmer evidently lived, that also was painted green. They passed by several of these houses during the afternoon, and sometimes people came to the doors and looked at them as if they would like to ask questions; but no one came near them nor spoke to them because of the great Lion, of which they were very much afraid. The people were all dressed in clothing of a lovely emerald-green color and wore peaked hats like those of **the Munchkins**.

"This must be the Land of Oz," said Dorothy, "and we are surely getting near the Emerald City."

"Yes," answered **the Scarecrow**. "Everything is green here, while in the country of the Munchkins blue was the favorite color. But the people do not seem to be as friendly as the Munchkins, and I'm afraid we shall be unable to find a place to pass the night."

"I should like something to eat besides fruit," said the girl, "and I'm sure **Toto** is nearly starved. Let us stop at the next house and talk to the people."

So, when they came to a good-sized farmhouse, Dorothy walked boldly up to the door and knocked.

A woman opened it just far enough to look out, and said, "What do you want, child, and why is that great Lion with you?"

"We wish to pass the night with you, if you will allow us," answered Dorothy; "and the Lion is my friend and comrade, and would not hurt you for the world."

"Is he tame?" asked the woman, opening the door a little wider.

"Oh, yes," said the girl, "and he is a great coward, too. He will be more afraid of you than you are of him."

"Well," said the woman, after thinking it over and taking another peep at the Lion, "if that is the case you may come in, and I will give you some supper and a place to sleep."

So they all entered the house, where there were, besides the woman, **two children and a man**. The man had hurt his leg, and was lying on the couch in a corner. They seemed greatly surprised to see so strange a company, and while the woman was busy laying the table the man asked:

"Where are you all going?"

"To the Emerald City," said Dorothy, "to see the Great Oz."

"Oh, indeed!" exclaimed the man. "Are you sure that Oz will see you?"

"Why not?" she replied.

"Why, it is said that he never lets anyone come into his presence. I have been to the Emerald City many times, and it is a beautiful and wonderful place; but I have never been permitted to see the Great Oz, nor do I know of any living person who has seen him."

"Does he never go out?" asked the Scarecrow.

"Never. He sits day after day in the great Throne Room of his Palace, and even those who wait upon him do not see him face to face."

"What is he like?" asked the girl.

"That is hard to tell," said the man thoughtfully. "You see, Oz is a Great Wizard, and can take on any form he wishes. So that some say he looks like a bird; and some say he looks like an elephant; and some say he looks like a cat. To others he appears as a beautiful fairy, or a brownie, or in any other form that pleases him. But who the real Oz is, when he is in his own form, no living person can tell."

"That is very strange," said Dorothy, "but we must try, in some way, to see him, or we shall have made our journey for nothing."

"Why do you wish to see the terrible Oz?" asked the man.

"I want him to give me some brains," said the Scarecrow eagerly.

"Oh, Oz could do that easily enough," declared the man. "He has more brains than he needs."

"And I want him to give me a heart," said the Tin Woodman.

"That will not trouble him," continued the man, "for Oz has a large collection of hearts, of all sizes and shapes."

"And I want him to give me courage," said the Cowardly Lion.

"Oz keeps a great pot of courage in his Throne Room," said the man, "which he has covered with a golden plate, to keep it from running over. He will be glad to give you some."

"And I want him to send me back to Kansas," said Dorothy.

"Where is Kansas?" asked the man, with surprise.

"I don't know," replied Dorothy sorrowfully, "but it is my home, and I'm sure it's somewhere."

"Very likely. Well, Oz can do anything; so I suppose he will find Kansas for you. But first you must get to see him, and that will be a hard task; for the Great Wizard does not like to see anyone, and he usually has his own way. But what do YOU want?" he continued, speaking to Toto. Toto only wagged his tail; for, strange to say, he could not speak.

The woman now called to them that supper was ready, so they gathered around the table and Dorothy ate some delicious porridge and a dish of scrambled eggs and a plate of nice white bread, and enjoyed her meal. The Lion ate some of the porridge, but did not care for it, saying it was made from oats and oats were food for horses, not for lions. The Scarecrow and the Tin Woodman ate nothing at all. Toto ate a little of everything, and was glad to get a good supper again.

The woman now gave Dorothy a bed to sleep in, and Toto lay down beside her, while the Lion guarded the door of her room so she might not be disturbed. The Scarecrow and the Tin Woodman stood up in a corner and kept quiet all night, although of course they could not sleep.

The next morning, as soon as the sun was up, they started on their way, and soon saw a beautiful green glow in the sky just before them.

"That must be the Emerald City," said Dorothy.

As they walked on, the green glow became brighter and brighter, and it seemed that at last they were nearing the end of their travels. Yet it was afternoon before they came to the great wall that surrounded the City. It was high and thick and of a bright green color.

In front of them, and at the end of the road of yellow brick, was a big gate, all studded with emeralds that glittered so in the sun that even the painted eyes of the Scarecrow were dazzled by their brilliancy.

There was a bell beside the gate, and Dorothy pushed the button and heard a silvery tinkle sound within. Then the big gate swung slowly open, and they all passed through and found themselves in a high arched room, the walls of which glistened with countless emeralds.

Before them stood **a little man** about the same size as the

Munchkins. He was clothed all in green, from his head to his feet, and even his skin was of a greenish tint. At his side was a large green box.

When he saw Dorothy and her companions the man asked, "What do you wish in the Emerald City?"

"We came here to see the Great Oz," said Dorothy.

The man was so surprised at this answer that he sat down to think it over.

"It has been many years since anyone asked me to see Oz," he said, shaking his head in perplexity. "He is powerful and terrible, and if you come on an idle or foolish errand to bother the wise reflections of the Great Wizard, he might be angry and destroy you all in an instant."

"But it is not a foolish errand, nor an idle one," replied the Scarecrow; "it is important. And we have been told that Oz is a good Wizard."

"So he is," said the green man, "and he rules the Emerald City wisely and well. But to those who are not honest, or who approach him from curiosity, he is most terrible, and few have ever dared ask to see his face. I am the Guardian of the Gates, and since you demand to see the Great Oz I must take you to his Palace. But first you must put on the spectacles."

"Why?" asked Dorothy.

"Because if you did not wear spectacles the brightness and glory of the Emerald City would blind you. Even those who live in the City must wear spectacles night and day. They are all locked on, for Oz so ordered it when the City was first built, and I have the only key that will unlock them."

He opened the big box, and Dorothy saw that it was filled with spectacles of every size and shape. All of them had green glasses in them. The Guardian of the Gates found a pair that would just fit Dorothy and put them over her eyes. There were two golden bands fastened to them that passed around the back of her head, where they were locked together by a little key that was at the end of a chain the Guardian of the Gates wore around his neck. When they were on, Dorothy could not take them off had she wished, but of course she did not wish to be blinded by the glare of the Emerald City, so she said nothing.

Then the green man fitted spectacles for the Scarecrow and the Tin Woodman and the Lion, and even on little Toto; and all were locked fast with the key.

Then the Guardian of the Gates put on his own glasses and told them he was ready to show them to the Palace. Taking a big golden key from a peg on the wall, he opened another gate, and they all followed him through the portal into the streets of the Emerald City.

STORY EVENT

A Story Event is an active change of a universal human value for one or more characters as a result of conflict (one character's desires clash with another's, or an environmental shift changes the universal human value).

A Working Scene contains at least one Story Event. To determine a scene's Story Event, answer these four Socratic questions:

1. The Action Story Component: What are the characters literally doing—that is, what are their micro on-the-surface actions?

The group makes their way all the way to the Emerald City, where they meet the Guardian of the Gates.

2. The Worldview Story Component: What is the essential tactic of the characters—that is, what above-the-surface macro behaviors are they employing that are linked to a universal human value?

Dorothy gets strangers on their side, a local family provides them food, shelter and information, and the Guardian of the Gates outfits them to enter the city.

3. The Heroic Journey 2.0 Component: What beyond-the-surface universal human values have changed for one or more characters in the scene? Which one of those value changes is most important and should be included in the Story Grid Spreadsheet?

The group collects a substantial amount of information in this scene and learns how to behave in the Emerald City.

When in doubt, the Story Grid rule of thumb is to highlight the value that best aligns with the progress of the global human value at stake in the story. *The Wonderful Wizard of Oz* is an Action Story, which has a global value at stake of Life/Death. Throughout the Story Grid

Spreadsheet, we'll track the ways life is threatened or enhanced scene by scene.

Uninformed to Informed

4. The Scene Event Synthesis: What Story Event sums up the scene's on-the-surface actions, essential above-the-surface worldview behavioral tactics, and beyond-the-surface value change? We will enter that event in the Story Grid Spreadsheet.

The group makes it to the Emerald City and meets the Guardian of the Gates, who informs them that they must wear spectacles when they are in the city.

HOW THE SCENE ABIDES BY THE FIVE COMMANDMENTS OF STORYTELLING

Inciting Incident: The group needs a place to spend the night and get dinner.

Turning Point Progressive Complication: The Guardian of the Gates informs the group that they must wear spectacles in the Emerald City.

Crisis: Best bad choice. If the group puts on the glasses as is required, they won't be able to get them off. If they don't put them on, they won't be allowed inside the city.

Climax: The group puts on the glasses.

Resolution: The Guardian of the Gates takes them inside the city limits and will lead them to Oz's palace.

11

THE WONDERFUL CITY OF OZ

SCENE ii

Even with eyes protected by the green spectacles, **Dorothy** and **her friends** were at first dazzled by the brilliancy of the wonderful City. The streets were lined with beautiful houses all built of green marble and studded everywhere with sparkling emeralds. They walked over a pavement of the same green marble, and where the blocks were joined together were rows of emeralds, set closely, and glittering in the brightness of the sun. The window panes were of green glass; even the sky above the City had a green tint, and the rays of the sun were green.

There were **many people**—men, women, and children—walking about, and these were all dressed in green clothes and had greenish skins. They looked at Dorothy and her strangely assorted company with wondering eyes, and **the children** all ran away and hid behind **their mothers** when they saw **the Lion**; but no one spoke to them. Many shops stood in the street, and Dorothy saw that everything in them was green. Green candy and green pop corn were offered for sale, as well as green shoes, green hats, and green clothes of all sorts. At one place a man was selling green lemonade, and when the children bought it Dorothy could see that they paid for it with green pennies.

There seemed to be no horses nor animals of any kind; the men carried things around in little green carts, which they pushed before them. Everyone seemed happy and contented and prosperous.

The Guardian of the Gates led them through the streets until they came to a big building, exactly in the middle of the City, which was the Palace of Oz, the Great Wizard. There was **a soldier** before the door, dressed in a green uniform and wearing a long green beard.

"Here are strangers," said the Guardian of the Gates to him, "and they demand to see the Great Oz."

"Step inside," answered the soldier, "and I will carry your message to him."

So they passed through the Palace Gates and were led into a big room with a green carpet and lovely green furniture set with emeralds. The soldier made them all wipe their feet upon a green mat before entering this room, and when they were seated he said politely:

"Please make yourselves comfortable while I go to the door of the Throne Room and tell Oz you are here."

They had to wait a long time before the soldier returned. When, at last, he came back, Dorothy asked:

"Have you seen Oz?"

"Oh, no," returned the soldier; "I have never seen him. But I spoke to him **as he sat behind his screen** and gave him your message. He said he will grant you an audience, if you so desire; but **each one of you must enter his presence alone**, and he will admit but one each day. Therefore, as you must remain in the Palace for several days, I will have you shown to rooms where you may rest in comfort after your journey."

"Thank you," replied the girl; "that is very kind of Oz."

The soldier now blew upon a green whistle, and at once **a young girl**, dressed in a pretty green silk gown, entered the room. She had lovely green hair and green eyes, and she bowed low before Dorothy as she said, "Follow me and I will show you your room."

So Dorothy said good-bye to all her friends except **Toto**, and taking the dog in her arms followed the green girl through seven passages and up three flights of stairs until they came to a room at the front of the Palace. It was the sweetest little room in the world, with a soft comfortable bed that had sheets of green silk and a green velvet counterpane. There was a tiny fountain in the middle of the room, **that** shot a spray of green perfume into the air, to fall back into a beautifully carved green marble basin. Beautiful green flowers stood in the windows, and there was a shelf with a row of little green books. When Dorothy had time to open these books she found them full of queer green pictures that made her laugh, they were so funny.

In a wardrobe were many green dresses, made of silk and satin and velvet; and all of them fitted Dorothy exactly.

"Make yourself perfectly at home," said the green girl, "and if you wish for anything ring the bell. Oz will send for you tomorrow morning."

She left Dorothy alone and went back to the others. These she also led to rooms, and each one of them found himself lodged in a very pleasant part of the Palace. Of course this politeness was wasted on the Scarecrow; for when he found himself alone in his room he stood stupidly in one spot, just within the doorway, to wait till morning. It would not rest him to lie down, and he could not close his eyes; so he remained all night staring at a little spider which was weaving its web in a corner of the room, just as if it were not one of the most wonderful rooms in the world. The Tin Woodman lay down on his bed from force of habit, for he remembered when he was made of flesh; but not being able to sleep, he passed the night moving his joints up and down to make sure they kept in good working order. The Lion would have preferred a bed of dried leaves in the forest, and did not like being shut up in a room; but he had too much sense to let this worry him, so he sprang upon the bed and rolled himself up like a cat and purred himself asleep in a minute.

The next morning, after breakfast, the green maiden came to fetch Dorothy, and she dressed her in one of the prettiest gowns, made of green brocaded satin. Dorothy put on a green silk apron and tied a green ribbon around Toto's neck, and they started for the Throne Room of the Great Oz.

First they came to a great hall in which were many ladies and gentlemen of the court, all dressed in rich costumes. These people had nothing to do but talk to each other, but they always came to wait outside the Throne Room every morning, although they were never permitted to see Oz. As Dorothy entered they looked at her curiously, and one of them whispered:

"Are you really going to look upon the face of Oz the Terrible?"

"Of course," answered the girl, "if he will see me."

"Oh, he will see you," said the soldier who had taken her message to the Wizard, "although he does not like to have people ask to see him. Indeed, at first he was angry and said I should send you back where you came from. Then he asked me what you looked like, and when I mentioned your **silver shoes** he was very much interested. At last I told him about **the mark upon your forehead**, and he decided he would admit you to his presence." (*This information sets up that Oz may believe that Dorothy is a "witch" and could in fact help him as opposed to him helping her.*)

Just then a bell rang, and the green girl said to Dorothy, "That is the signal. You must go into the Throne Room alone."

She opened a little door and Dorothy walked boldly through and found herself in a wonderful place. It was a big, round room with a high arched roof, and the walls and ceiling and floor were covered with large emeralds set closely together. In the center of the roof was a great light, as bright as the sun, which made the emeralds sparkle in a wonderful manner.

But what interested Dorothy most was the big throne of green marble that stood in the middle of the room. It was shaped like a chair and sparkled with gems, as did everything else. **In the center of the chair was an enormous Head, without a body to support it or any arms or legs whatever.** There was no hair upon this head, but it had eyes and a nose and mouth, and was much bigger than the head of the biggest giant.

As Dorothy gazed upon this in wonder and fear, the eyes turned slowly and looked at her sharply and steadily. Then the mouth moved, and Dorothy heard a voice say:

"I am Oz, the Great and Terrible. Who are you, and why do you seek me?"

It was not such an awful voice as she had expected to come from the big Head; so she took courage and answered:

"I am Dorothy, the Small and Meek. I have come to you for help."

The eyes looked at her thoughtfully for a full minute. Then said the voice:

"Where did you get the silver shoes?"

"I got them from **the Wicked Witch of the East,** when my house fell on her and killed her," she replied.

"Where did you get the mark upon your forehead?" continued the voice.

"That is where the **Good Witch of the North** kissed me when she bade me good-bye and sent me to you," said the girl.

Again the eyes looked at her sharply, and they saw she was telling the truth. Then Oz asked, "What do you wish me to do?"

"Send me back to Kansas, where my **Aunt Em** and **Uncle Henry** are," she answered earnestly. "I don't like your country, although it is so beautiful. And I am sure Aunt Em will be dreadfully worried over my being away so long."

The eyes winked three times, and then they turned up to the ceiling and down to the floor and rolled around so queerly that they seemed to see every part of the room. And at last they looked at Dorothy again.

"Why should I do this for you?" asked Oz.

"Because you are strong and I am weak; because you are a Great Wizard and I am only a little girl."

"But you were strong enough to kill the Wicked Witch of the East," said Oz.

"That just happened," returned Dorothy simply; "I could not help it."

"Well," said the Head, "I will give you my answer. You have no right to expect me to send you back to Kansas unless you do something for me in return. In this country everyone must pay for everything he gets. If you wish me to use my magic power to send you home again you must do something for me first. **Help me and I will help you.**" (*Quid Pro Quo*)

"What must I do?" asked the girl.

"Kill **the Wicked Witch of the West**," answered Oz.

"But I cannot!" exclaimed Dorothy, greatly surprised.

"You killed the Witch of the East and you wear the silver shoes, which bear a powerful charm. There is now but one Wicked Witch left in all this land, and when you can tell me she is dead I will send you back to Kansas—but not before."

The little girl began to weep, she was so much disappointed; and the eyes winked again and looked upon her anxiously, **as if the Great Oz felt that she could help him if she would.**

"I never killed anything, willingly," she sobbed. "Even if I wanted to, how could I kill the Wicked Witch? If you, who are Great and Terrible, cannot kill her yourself, how do you expect me to do it?"

"I do not know," said the Head; "but that is my answer, and until the Wicked Witch dies you will not see your uncle and aunt again. Remember that the Witch is Wicked—tremendously Wicked—and ought to be killed. Now go, and do not ask to see me again until you have done your task."

Sorrowfully Dorothy left the Throne Room and went back where the Lion and the Scarecrow and the Tin Woodman were waiting to hear what Oz had said to her. "There is no hope for me," she said sadly, "for **Oz will not send me home until I have killed the Wicked Witch of the West; and that I can never do.**"

Her friends were sorry, but could do nothing to help her; so Dorothy went to her own room and lay down on the bed and cried herself to sleep.

The next morning the soldier with the green whiskers came to the Scarecrow and said:

"Come with me, for Oz has sent for you."

So the Scarecrow followed him and was admitted into the great Throne Room, where he saw, sitting in the emerald throne, **a most lovely Lady.** She was dressed in green silk gauze and wore upon her flowing green locks a crown of jewels. Growing from her shoulders were wings, gorgeous in color and so light that they fluttered if the slightest breath of air reached them.

When the Scarecrow had bowed, as prettily as his straw stuffing would let him, before this beautiful creature, she looked upon him sweetly, and said:

"I am Oz, the Great and Terrible. Who are you, and why do you seek me?"

Now the Scarecrow, who had expected to see the great Head

Dorothy had told him of, was much astonished; but he answered her bravely.

"I am only a Scarecrow, stuffed with straw. Therefore I have no brains, and I come to you praying that you will put brains in my head instead of straw, so that I may become as much a man as any other in your dominions."

"Why should I do this for you?" asked the Lady.

"Because you are wise and powerful, and no one else can help me," answered the Scarecrow.

"I never grant favors without some return," said Oz; "but this much I will promise. If you will kill for me the Wicked Witch of the West, I will bestow upon you a great many brains, and such good brains that you will be the wisest man in all the Land of Oz."

"I thought you asked Dorothy to kill the Witch," said the Scarecrow, in surprise.

"So I did. I don't care who kills her. But until she is dead I will not grant your wish. Now go, and do not seek me again until you have earned the brains you so greatly desire."

The Scarecrow went sorrowfully back to his friends and told them what Oz had said; and Dorothy was surprised to find that the Great Wizard was not a Head, as she had seen him, but a lovely Lady.

"All the same," said the Scarecrow, "she needs a heart as much as the Tin Woodman."

On the next morning the soldier with the green whiskers came to the Tin Woodman and said:

"Oz has sent for you. Follow me."

So the Tin Woodman followed him and came to the great Throne Room. He did not know whether he would find Oz a lovely Lady or a Head, but he hoped it would be the lovely Lady. "For," he said to himself, "if it is the head, I am sure I shall not be given a heart, since a head has no heart of its own and therefore cannot feel for me. But if it is the lovely Lady I shall beg hard for a heart, for all ladies are themselves said to be kindly hearted."

But when the Woodman entered the great Throne Room he saw neither the Head nor the Lady, for Oz had taken the shape of **a most terrible Beast**. It was nearly as big as an elephant, and the green throne seemed hardly strong enough to hold its weight. The Beast had a head like that of a rhinoceros, only there were five eyes in its face. There were five long arms growing out of its body, and it also had five long, slim legs. Thick, woolly hair covered every part of it, and a more dreadful-looking monster could not be imagined. It was fortunate the Tin Woodman had no heart at that moment, for it would have beat loud and fast from terror. But being only tin, the Woodman was not at all afraid, although he was much disappointed.

"I am Oz, the Great and Terrible," spoke the Beast, in a voice that was one great roar. "Who are you, and why do you seek me?"

"I am a Woodman, and made of tin. Therefore I have no heart, and cannot love. I pray you to give me a heart that I may be as other men are."

"Why should I do this?" demanded the Beast.

"Because I ask it, and you alone can grant my request," answered the Woodman.

Oz gave a low growl at this, but said, gruffly: "If you indeed desire a heart, you must earn it."

"How?" asked the Woodman.

"Help Dorothy to kill the Wicked Witch of the West," replied the Beast. "When the Witch is dead, come to me, and I will then give you the biggest and kindest and most loving heart in all the Land of Oz."

So the Tin Woodman was forced to return sorrowfully to his friends and tell them of the terrible Beast he had seen. They all wondered greatly at the many forms the Great Wizard could take upon himself, and the Lion said:

"If he is a Beast when I go to see him, I shall roar my loudest, and so frighten him that he will grant all I ask. And if he is the lovely Lady, I shall pretend to spring upon her, and so compel her to do my bidding. And if he is the great Head, he will be at my mercy; for I will roll this head all about the room until he promises to give us what we desire. So be of good cheer, my friends, for all will yet be well."

The next morning the soldier with the green whiskers led the Lion to the great Throne Room and bade him enter the presence of Oz.

The Lion at once passed through the door, and glancing around saw, to his surprise, that before the throne was a Ball of Fire, so fierce and glowing he could scarcely bear to gaze upon it. His first thought was that Oz had by accident caught on fire and was burning up; but when he tried to go nearer, the heat was so intense that it singed his whiskers, and he crept back tremblingly to a spot nearer the door.

Then a low, quiet voice came from the Ball of Fire, and these were the words it spoke:

"I am Oz, the Great and Terrible. Who are you, and why do you seek me?"

And the Lion answered, "I am a Cowardly Lion, afraid of everything. I came to you to beg that you give me courage, so that in reality I may become the King of Beasts, as men call me."

"Why should I give you courage?" demanded Oz.

"Because of all Wizards you are the greatest, and alone have power to grant my request," answered the Lion.

The Ball of Fire burned fiercely for a time, and the voice said, "Bring me proof that the Wicked Witch is dead, and that moment I will give you courage. But as long as the Witch lives, you must remain a coward."

The Lion was angry at this speech, but could say nothing in reply, and while he stood silently gazing at the Ball of Fire it became so furiously hot that he turned tail and rushed from the room. He was glad to find his friends waiting for him, and told them of his terrible interview with the Wizard.

"What shall we do now?" asked Dorothy sadly.

"There is only one thing we can do," returned the Lion, "and that is to go to the land of **the Winkies**, seek out the Wicked Witch, and destroy her."

"But suppose we cannot?" said the girl.

"Then I shall never have courage," declared the Lion.

"And I shall never have brains," added the Scarecrow.

"And I shall never have a heart," spoke the Tin Woodman.

"And I shall never see Aunt Em and Uncle Henry," said Dorothy, beginning to cry.

"Be careful!" cried the green girl. "The tears will fall on your green silk gown and spot it."

So Dorothy dried her eyes and said, "I suppose we must try it; but I am sure I do not want to kill anybody, even to see Aunt Em again."

"I will go with you; but I'm too much of a coward to kill the Witch," said the Lion.

"I will go too," declared the Scarecrow; "but I shall not be of much help to you, I am such a fool."

"I haven't the heart to harm even a Witch," remarked the Tin Woodman; "but if you go I certainly shall go with you."

Therefore it was decided to start upon their journey **the next morning**, and the Woodman sharpened his axe on a green grindstone and had all his joints properly oiled. The Scarecrow stuffed himself with fresh straw and Dorothy put new paint on his eyes that he might see better. The green girl, who was very kind to them, filled Dorothy's basket with good things to eat, and fastened a little bell around Toto's neck with a green ribbon.

They went to bed quite early and slept soundly until daylight, when they were awakened by the crowing of a green cock that lived in the back yard of the Palace, and the cackling of a hen that had laid a green egg.

STORY EVENT

A Story Event is an active change of a universal human value for one or more characters as a result of conflict (one character's desires clash with another's, or an environmental shift changes the universal human value).

A Working Scene contains at least one Story Event. To determine a scene's Story Event, answer these four Socratic questions:

1. The Action Story Component: What are the characters literally doing—that is, what are their micro on-the-surface actions?

Each member of the group meets separately with Oz.

2. The Worldview Story Component: What is the essential tactic of the characters—that is, what above-the-surface macro behaviors are they employing that are linked to a universal human value?

Each member of the group humbles themselves in the presence of Oz in order to induce his benevolence.

3. The Heroic Journey 2.0 Component: What beyond-the-surface universal human values have changed for one or more characters in the scene? Which one of those value changes is most important and should be included in the Story Grid Spreadsheet?

Each member of the group has deep hope that Oz will look upon them kindly and grant their wishes without requiring an unreasonable quid pro quo, but each discovers that Oz never grants favors without some return.

When in doubt, the Story Grid rule of thumb is to highlight the value that best aligns with the progress of the global human value at stake in the story. *The Wonderful Wizard of Oz* is an Action Story, which has a global value at stake of Life/Death. Throughout the Story Grid

Spreadsheet, we'll track the ways life is threatened or enhanced scene by scene.

Hope to Despair

4. The Scene Event Synthesis: What Story Event sums up the scene's on-the-surface actions, essential above-the-surface worldview behavioral tactics, and beyond-the-surface value change? We will enter that event in the Story Grid Spreadsheet.

The four friends see Oz individually, and he tells each of them that he won't grant any of their wishes until they kill the Wicked Witch of the West.

HOW THE SCENE ABIDES BY THE FIVE COMMANDMENTS OF STORYTELLING

Inciting Incident: The group is granted an audience with Oz.

Turning Point Progressive Complication: Oz wants a quid pro quo. They have to kill the Wicked Witch of the West to get him to help them.

Crisis: Irreconcilable Goods: If they agree to kill the Wicked Witch to get what they want, the Witch will die and they will become cold-blooded killers.

Climax: The group reluctantly decides to set off on the mission.

Resolution: The next morning the group leaves the Emerald City.

12

THE SEARCH FOR THE WICKED WITCH

SCENE 12

The soldier with the green whiskers led them through the streets of the Emerald City until they reached the room where **the Guardian of the Gates** lived. This officer unlocked their spectacles to put them back in his great box, and then he politely opened the gate for **our friends.** (*This reminder of the third person omniscient narration is perhaps a way in which to remind children that this is a make-believe story.*)

"Which road leads to **the Wicked Witch of the West?**" asked **Dorothy.**

"There is no road," answered the Guardian of the Gates. "No one ever wishes to go that way."

"How, then, are we to find her?" inquired the girl.

"That will be easy," replied the man, "for when she knows you are in the country of **the Winkies** she will find you, and make you all her slaves."

"Perhaps not," said **the Scarecrow,** "for we mean to destroy her."

"Oh, that is different," said the Guardian of the Gates. "No one has ever destroyed her before, so I naturally thought she would make slaves of you, as she has of the rest. But take care; for she is wicked and fierce, and may not allow you to destroy her. Keep to the West, where the sun sets, and you cannot fail to find her."

They thanked him and bade him good-bye, and turned toward the West, walking over fields of soft grass dotted here and there with daisies and buttercups. Dorothy still wore the pretty silk dress she had put on in the palace, but now, to her surprise, she found **it was no longer green, but pure white**. The ribbon around Toto's neck had also lost its green color and was as white as Dorothy's dress.

The Emerald City was soon left far behind. As they advanced the ground became rougher and hillier, for there were no farms nor houses in this country of the West, and the ground was untilled.

In the afternoon the sun shone hot in their faces, for there were no trees to offer them shade; so that before night Dorothy and **Toto** and the **Lion** were tired, and lay down upon the grass and fell asleep, with **the Woodman** and **the Scarecrow** keeping watch.

Now **the Wicked Witch of the West** had but one eye, yet that was as powerful as a telescope, and could see everywhere. So, as she sat in the door of her castle, she happened to look around and saw Dorothy lying asleep, with her friends all about her. They were a long distance off, but the Wicked Witch was angry to find them in her country; so she blew upon a silver whistle that hung around her neck.

At once there came running to her from all directions **a pack of great wolves**. They had long legs and fierce eyes and sharp teeth.

"Go to those people," said the Witch, "and tear them to pieces."

"Are you not going to make them your slaves?" asked **the leader of the wolves**.

"No," she answered, "one is of tin, and one of straw; one is a girl and another a Lion. None of them is fit to work, so you may tear them into small pieces."

"Very well," said the wolf, and he dashed away at full speed, followed by the others.

It was lucky the Scarecrow and the Woodman were wide awake and heard the wolves coming.

"This is my fight," said the Woodman, "so get behind me and I will meet them as they come."

He seized his axe, which he had made very sharp, and as the

leader of the wolves came on the Tin Woodman swung his arm and chopped the wolf's head from its body, so that it immediately died. As soon as he could raise his axe another wolf came up, and he also fell under the sharp edge of the Tin Woodman's weapon. There were **forty wolves**, and forty times a wolf was killed, so that at last they all lay dead in a heap before the Woodman.

Then he put down his axe and sat beside the Scarecrow, who said, "It was a good fight, friend."

They waited until Dorothy awoke the next morning. The little girl was quite frightened when she saw the great pile of shaggy wolves, but the Tin Woodman told her all. She thanked him for saving them and sat down to breakfast, after which they started again upon their journey.

Now this same morning the Wicked Witch came to the door of her castle and looked out with her one eye that could see far off. She saw all her wolves lying dead, and the strangers still traveling through her country. This made her angrier than before, and she blew her silver whistle twice.

Straightway **a great flock of wild crows** came flying toward her, enough to darken the sky.

And the Wicked Witch said to the **King Crow**, "Fly at once to the strangers; peck out their eyes and tear them to pieces."

The wild crows flew in one great flock toward Dorothy and her companions. When the little girl saw them coming she was afraid.

But the Scarecrow said, "This is my battle, so lie down beside me and you will not be harmed."

So they all lay upon the ground except the Scarecrow, and he stood up and stretched out his arms. And when the crows saw him they were frightened, as these birds always are by scarecrows, and did not dare to come any nearer. But the King Crow said:

"It is only a stuffed man. I will peck his eyes out."

The King Crow flew at the Scarecrow, who caught it by the head and twisted its neck until it died. And then another crow flew at him, and the Scarecrow twisted its neck also. There were **forty crows**, and forty times the Scarecrow twisted a neck, until at last all were lying

95

dead beside him. Then he called to his companions to rise, and again they went upon their journey.

When the Wicked Witch looked out again and saw all her crows lying in a heap, she got into a terrible rage, and blew three times upon her silver whistle.

Forthwith there was heard a great buzzing in the air, and a swarm of black bees came flying toward her.

"Go to the strangers and sting them to death!" commanded the Witch, and the bees turned and flew rapidly until they came to where Dorothy and her friends were walking. But the Woodman had seen them coming, and the Scarecrow had decided what to do.

"Take out my straw and scatter it over the little girl and the dog and the Lion," he said to the Woodman, "and the bees cannot sting them." This the Woodman did, and as Dorothy lay close beside the Lion and held Toto in her arms, the straw covered them entirely.

The bees came and found no one but the Woodman to sting, so they flew at him and broke off all their stings against the tin, without hurting the Woodman at all. And as bees cannot live when their stings are broken that was the end of the black bees, and they lay scattered thick about the Woodman, like little heaps of fine coal.

Then Dorothy and the Lion got up, and the girl helped the Tin Woodman put the straw back into the Scarecrow again, until he was as good as ever. So they started upon their journey once more.

The Wicked Witch was so angry when she saw her black bees in little heaps like fine coal that she stamped her foot and tore her hair and gnashed her teeth. And then she called **a dozen of her slaves**, who were the Winkies, and gave them sharp spears, telling them to go to the strangers and destroy them.

The Winkies were not a brave people, but they had to do as they were told. So they marched away until they came near to Dorothy. Then the Lion gave a great roar and sprang towards them, and the poor Winkies were so frightened that they ran back as fast as they could.

When they returned to the castle the Wicked Witch beat them well with a strap, and sent them back to their work, after which she sat down to think what she should do next. She could not understand how all her plans to destroy these strangers had failed; but she was a powerful Witch, as well as a wicked one, and she soon made up her mind how to act.

There was, in her cupboard, **a Golden Cap**, with a circle of diamonds and rubies running round it. This Golden Cap had a charm. Whoever owned it could call **three times** upon **the Winged Monkeys**, who would obey any order they were given. But no person could command these strange creatures more than three times. Twice already the Wicked Witch had used the charm of the Cap. Once was when she had made the Winkies her slaves, and set herself to rule over their country. The Winged Monkeys had helped her do this. The second time was when she had fought against the Great Oz himself, and driven him out of the land of the West. The Winged Monkeys had also helped her in doing this. Only once more could she use this Golden Cap, for which reason she did not like to do so until all her other powers were exhausted. But now that her fierce wolves and her wild crows and her stinging bees were gone, and her slaves had been scared away by the Cowardly Lion, she saw there was only one way left to destroy Dorothy and her friends.

So the Wicked Witch took the Golden Cap from her cupboard and placed it upon her head. Then she stood upon her left foot and said slowly:

"Ep-pe, pep-pe, kak-ke!"

Next she stood upon her right foot and said:

"Hil-lo, hol-lo, hel-lo!"

After this she stood upon both feet and cried in a loud voice:

"Ziz-zy, zuz-zy, zik!"

Now the charm began to work. The sky was darkened, and a low rumbling sound was heard in the air. There was a rushing of many wings, a great chattering and laughing, and the sun came out of the dark sky to show the Wicked Witch surrounded by a crowd of monkeys, each with a pair of immense and powerful wings on his shoulders.

One, much bigger than the others, seemed to be their leader. He flew close to the Witch and said, "You have called us for the third and last time. What do you command?"

"Go to the strangers who are within my land and destroy them all except the Lion," said the Wicked Witch. "Bring that beast to me, for I have a mind to harness him like a horse, and make him work."

"Your commands shall be obeyed," said the leader. Then, with a great deal of chattering and noise, the Winged Monkeys flew away to the place where Dorothy and her friends were walking.

Some of the Monkeys seized the Tin Woodman and carried him through the air until they were over a country thickly covered with sharp rocks. Here they dropped the poor Woodman, who fell a great distance to the rocks, where he lay so battered and dented that he could neither move nor groan.

Others of the Monkeys caught the Scarecrow, and with their long fingers pulled all of the straw out of his clothes and head. They made his hat and boots and clothes into a small bundle and threw it into the top branches of a tall tree.

The remaining Monkeys threw pieces of stout rope around the Lion and wound many coils about his body and head and legs, until he was unable to bite or scratch or struggle in any way. Then they lifted him up and flew away with him to the Witch's castle, where he was placed in a small yard with a high iron fence around it, so that he could not escape.

But Dorothy they did not harm at all. She stood, with Toto in her arms, watching the sad fate of her comrades and thinking it would soon be her turn. The leader of the Winged Monkeys flew up to her, his long, hairy arms stretched out and his ugly face grinning terribly; **but he saw the mark of the Good Witch's kiss upon her forehead and stopped short, motioning the others not to touch her**.

"We dare not harm this little girl," he said to them, "for she is protected by **the Power of Good**, and **that is greater than the Power of Evil**. All we can do is to carry her to the castle of the Wicked Witch and leave her there."

So, carefully and gently, they lifted Dorothy in their arms and carried her swiftly through the air until they came to the castle, where they set her down upon the front doorstep. Then the leader said to the Witch:

"We have obeyed you as far as we were able. The Tin Woodman and the Scarecrow are destroyed, and the Lion is tied up in your yard. The little girl we dare not harm, nor the dog she carries in her arms.

Your power over our band is now ended, and you will never see us again."

Then all the Winged Monkeys, with much laughing and chattering and noise, flew into the air and were soon out of sight.

The Wicked Witch was both surprised and worried when she saw the mark on Dorothy's forehead, for she knew well that neither the Winged Monkeys nor she, herself, dare hurt the girl in any way. She looked down at Dorothy's feet, and seeing the Silver Shoes, began to tremble with fear, for she knew what a powerful charm belonged to them. At first the Witch was tempted to run away from Dorothy; but she happened to look into the child's eyes and saw how simple the soul behind them was, and that **the little girl did not know of the wonderful power the Silver Shoes gave her. So the Wicked Witch laughed to herself, and thought, "I can still make her my slave, for she does not know how to use her power."** Then she said to Dorothy, harshly and severely:

"Come with me; and see that you mind everything I tell you, for if you do not I will make an end of you, as I did of the Tin Woodman and the Scarecrow."

Dorothy followed her through many of the beautiful rooms in her castle until they came to the kitchen, where the Witch bade her clean the pots and kettles and sweep the floor and keep the fire fed with wood.

Dorothy went to work meekly, with her mind made up to work as hard as she could; for she was glad the Wicked Witch had decided not to kill her.

With Dorothy hard at work, the Witch thought she would go into the courtyard and harness the Cowardly Lion like a horse; it would amuse her, she was sure, to make him draw her chariot whenever she wished to go to drive. But as she opened the gate the Lion gave a loud roar and bounded at her so fiercely that the Witch was afraid, and ran out and shut the gate again.

"If I cannot harness you," said the Witch to the Lion, speaking through the bars of the gate, "I can starve you. You shall have nothing to eat until you do as I wish."

So after that she took no food to the imprisoned Lion; but every day she came to the gate at noon and asked, "Are you ready to be harnessed like a horse?"

And the Lion would answer, "No. If you come in this yard, I will bite you."

The reason the Lion did not have to do as the Witch wished was that every night, while the woman was asleep, Dorothy carried him food from the cupboard. After he had eaten he would lie down on his bed of straw, and Dorothy would lie beside him and put her head on his soft, shaggy mane, while they talked of their troubles and tried to plan some way to escape. But they could find no way to get out of the castle, for it was constantly guarded by **the yellow Winkies, who were the slaves of the Wicked Witch and too afraid of her not to do as she told them.**

The girl had to work hard during the day, and often the Witch threatened to beat her with the same old umbrella she always carried in her hand. But, in truth, she did not dare to strike Dorothy, because of the mark upon her forehead. The child did not know this, and was full of fear for herself and Toto. Once the Witch struck Toto a blow with her umbrella and the brave little dog flew at her and bit her leg in return. The Witch did not bleed where she was bitten, for she was so wicked that the blood in her had dried up many years before.

Dorothy's life became very sad as she grew to understand that it would be harder than ever to get back to Kansas and **Aunt Em** again. Sometimes she would cry bitterly for hours, with Toto sitting at her feet and looking into her face, whining dismally to show how sorry he was for his little mistress. Toto did not really care whether he was in Kansas or the Land of Oz so long as Dorothy was with him; but he knew the little girl was unhappy, and that made him unhappy too.

Now the Wicked Witch had a great longing to have for her own the Silver Shoes which the girl always wore. Her bees and her crows and her wolves were lying in heaps and drying up, and she had used up all the power of the Golden Cap; but if she could only get hold of the Silver Shoes, they would give her more power than all the other things she had lost. She watched Dorothy carefully, to see if she ever took off her shoes, thinking she might steal them. But the child was so proud of her pretty shoes that she never took them off except at night and when she took her bath. The Witch was too much afraid of the dark to dare go in Dorothy's room at night to take the shoes, and her dread of water was greater than her fear of the dark, so she never came near when Dorothy was bathing. Indeed, **the old Witch never touched water, nor ever let water touch her in any way.**

But the wicked creature was very cunning, and she finally thought of a trick that would give her what she wanted. She placed a bar of iron in the middle of the kitchen floor, and then by her magic arts made the iron invisible to human eyes. So that when Dorothy walked across the floor she stumbled over the bar, not being able to see it, and fell at full length. She was not much hurt, but in her fall one of the Silver Shoes came off; and before she could reach it, the Witch had snatched it away and put it on her own skinny foot.

The wicked woman was greatly pleased with the success of her trick, for as long as she had one of the shoes she owned half the power of their charm, and Dorothy could not use it against her, even had she known how to do so.

The little girl, seeing she had lost one of her pretty shoes, grew angry, and said to the Witch, "Give me back my shoe!"

"I will not," retorted the Witch, "for it is now my shoe, and not yours."

"You are a wicked creature!" cried Dorothy. "You have no right to take my shoe from me."

"I shall keep it, just the same," said the Witch, laughing at her, "and someday I shall get the other one from you, too."

This made Dorothy so very angry that she picked up the bucket of water that stood near and dashed it over the Witch, wetting her from head to foot.

Instantly the wicked woman gave a loud cry of fear, and then, as Dorothy looked at her in wonder, the Witch began to shrink and fall away.

"See what you have done!" she screamed. "In a minute I shall melt away."

"I'm very sorry, indeed," said Dorothy, who was truly frightened to see the Witch actually melting away like brown sugar before her very eyes.

"Didn't you know water would be the end of me?" asked the Witch, in a wailing, despairing voice.

"Of course not," answered Dorothy. "How should I?"

"Well, in a few minutes I shall be all melted, and you will have the castle to yourself. I have been wicked in my day, but I never thought a little girl like you would ever be able to melt me and end my wicked deeds. Look out—here I go!"

With these words the Witch fell down in a brown, melted, shapeless mass and began to spread over the clean boards of the kitchen floor. Seeing that she had really melted away to nothing, Dorothy drew another bucket of water and threw it over the mess. She then swept it all out the door. After picking out the silver shoe, which was all that was left of the old woman, she cleaned and dried it with a cloth, and put it on her foot again. Then, being at last free to do as she chose, she ran out to the courtyard to tell the Lion that the Wicked Witch of the West had come to an end, and that they were no longer prisoners in a strange land.

• ANALYZING THE SCENE •

STORY EVENT

A Story Event is an active change of a universal human value for one or more characters as a result of conflict (one character's desires clash with another's, or an environmental shift changes the universal human value).

A Working Scene contains at least one Story Event. To determine a scene's Story Event, answer these four Socratic questions:

1. The Action Story Component: What are the characters literally doing—that is, what are their micro on-the-surface actions?

The group makes their way into the territory of the Wicked Witch of the West.

2. The Worldview Story Component: What is the essential tactic of the characters—that is, what above-the-surface macro behaviors are they employing that are linked to a universal human value?

All of the group members release their inner shadows. They destroy in the service of a greater good. The Tin Woodman kills the wolves, the Scarecrow kills the crows, the Lion terrifies the Winkies and Dorothy slays the witch.

3. The Heroic Journey 2.0 Component: What beyond-the-surface universal human values have changed for one or more characters in the scene? Which one of those value changes is most important and should be included in the Story Grid Spreadsheet?

When in doubt, the Story Grid rule of thumb is to highlight the value that best aligns with the progress of the global human value at stake in the story. *The Wonderful Wizard of Oz* is an Action Story, which has a global value at stake of Life/Death. Throughout the Story Grid

Spreadsheet, we'll track the ways life is threatened or enhanced scene by scene.

The value shift is clear for the Scarecrow, Tin Woodman, and witch, *Life to Death*.

The value shift for Dorothy and the Lion moves from *Free to Imprisoned to Free*.

4. The Scene Event Synthesis: What Story Event sums up the scene's on-the-surface actions, essential above-the-surface worldview behavioral tactics, and beyond-the-surface value change? We will enter that event in the Story Grid Spreadsheet.

The group moves through the west, evading the witch's power, and eventually an angry Dorothy slays her by washing her away with a bucket of water.

HOW THE SCENE ABIDES BY THE FIVE COMMANDMENTS OF STORYTELLING

Inciting Incident: A pack of wolves attacks the group.

Turning Point Progressive Complication: The winged monkeys destroy the Tin Woodman and the Scarecrow and capture the Lion and Dorothy for the witch.

Crisis: Best bad choice. If Dorothy retaliates against the witch for stealing her shoe, she will serve the forces of destruction and not act out of "goodness." If she doesn't, the witch will attain more power.

Climax: Dorothy releases her anger and throws the water on the witch.

Resolution: The witch dies.

13

THE RESCUE

SCENE 13

The Cowardly Lion was much pleased to hear that **the Wicked Witch** had been melted by a bucket of water, and **Dorothy** at once unlocked the gate of his prison and set him free. They went in together to the castle, where Dorothy's first act was to call all **the Winkies** together and tell them that they were no longer slaves.

There was great rejoicing among the yellow Winkies, for they had been made to work hard during many years for the Wicked Witch, who had always treated them with great cruelty. They kept this day as a holiday, then and ever after, and spent the time in feasting and dancing.

"If our friends, **the Scarecrow** and **the Tin Woodman**, were only with us," said the Lion, "I should be quite happy."

"Don't you suppose we could rescue them?" asked the girl anxiously.

"We can try," answered the Lion.

So they called the yellow Winkies and asked them if they would help to rescue their friends, and the Winkies said that they would be delighted to do all in their power for Dorothy, who had set them free from bondage. So she chose a number of the Winkies who looked as if they knew the most, and they all started away. They traveled that day and part of the next until they came to the rocky plain where the Tin Woodman lay, all battered and bent. His axe was near him, but the blade was rusted and the handle broken off short.

The Winkies lifted him tenderly in their arms, and carried him back to the Yellow Castle again, Dorothy shedding a few tears by the way at the sad plight of her old friend, and the Lion looking sober and sorry. When they reached the castle Dorothy said to the Winkies:

"Are any of your people tinsmiths?"

"Oh, yes. Some of us are very good tinsmiths," they told her.

"Then bring them to me," she said. And when the tinsmiths came, bringing with them all their tools in baskets, she inquired, "Can you straighten out those dents in the Tin Woodman, and bend him back into shape again, and solder him together where he is broken?"

The tinsmiths looked the Woodman over carefully and then answered that they thought they could mend him so he would be as good as ever. So they set to work in one of the big yellow rooms of the castle and worked for three days and four nights, hammering and twisting and bending and soldering and polishing and pounding at the legs and body and head of the Tin Woodman, until at last he was straightened out into his old form, and his joints worked as well as ever. To be sure, there were several patches on him, but the tinsmiths did a good job, and as the Woodman was not a vain man he did not mind the patches at all.

When, at last, he walked into Dorothy's room and thanked her for rescuing him, he was so pleased that he wept tears of joy, and Dorothy had to wipe every tear carefully from his face with her apron, so his joints would not be rusted. At the same time her own tears fell thick and fast at the joy of meeting her old friend again, and these tears did not need to be wiped away. As for the Lion, he wiped his eyes so often with the tip of his tail that it became quite wet, and he was obliged to go out into the courtyard and hold it in the sun till it dried.

"If we only had the Scarecrow with us again," said the Tin Woodman, when Dorothy had finished telling him everything that had happened, "I should be quite happy."

"We must try to find him," said the girl.

So she called the Winkies to help her, and they walked all that day and part of the next until they came to the tall tree in the branches of which **the Winged Monkeys** had tossed the Scarecrow's clothes.

It was a very tall tree, and the trunk was so smooth that no one could climb it; but the Woodman said at once, "I'll chop it down, and then we can get the Scarecrow's clothes."

Now while the tinsmiths had been at work mending the Woodman himself, another of the Winkies, who was a goldsmith, had made an axe-handle of solid gold and fitted it to the Woodman's axe, instead of the old broken handle. Others polished the blade until all the rust was removed and it glistened like burnished silver.

As soon as he had spoken, the Tin Woodman began to chop, and in a short time the tree fell over with a crash, whereupon the Scarecrow's clothes fell out of the branches and rolled off on the ground.

Dorothy picked them up and had the Winkies carry them back to the castle, where they were stuffed with nice, clean straw; and behold! here was the Scarecrow, as good as ever, thanking them over and over again for saving him.

Now that they were reunited, Dorothy and her friends **spent a few happy days at the Yellow Castle**, where they found everything they needed to make them comfortable.

But one day the girl thought of **Aunt Em**, and said, "We must go back **to Oz**, and claim his promise."

"Yes," said the Woodman, "at last I shall get my heart."

"And I shall get my brains," added the Scarecrow joyfully.

"And I shall get my courage," said the Lion thoughtfully.

"And I shall get back to Kansas," cried Dorothy, clapping her hands. "Oh, let us start for the Emerald City tomorrow!"

This they decided to do. The next day they called the Winkies together and bade them good-bye. The Winkies were sorry to have them go, and they had grown so fond of the Tin Woodman that they begged him to stay and rule over them and the Yellow Land of the West. Finding they were determined to go, the Winkies gave **Toto** and the Lion each a golden collar; and to Dorothy they presented a beautiful bracelet studded with diamonds; and to the Scarecrow they gave a gold-headed walking stick, to keep him from stumbling; and to the Tin

Woodman they offered a silver oil-can, inlaid with gold and set with precious jewels. (*Gifts for succeeding in freeing the Winkies*)

Every one of the travelers made the Winkies a pretty speech in return, and all shook hands with them until their arms ached.

Dorothy went to the Witch's cupboard to fill her basket with food for the journey, and there she saw **the Golden Cap.** She tried it on her own head and found that it fitted her exactly. She did not know anything about the charm of the Golden Cap, but she saw that it was pretty, so she made up her mind to wear it and carry her sunbonnet in the basket.

Then, being prepared for the journey, they all started for the Emerald City; and the Winkies gave them three cheers and many good wishes to carry with them.

• ANALYZING THE SCENE •

STORY EVENT

A Story Event is an active change of a universal human value for one or more characters as a result of conflict (one character's desires clash with another's, or an environmental shift changes the universal human value).

A Working Scene contains at least one Story Event. To determine a scene's Story Event, answer these four Socratic questions:

1. The Action Story Component: What are the characters literally doing—that is, what are their micro on-the-surface actions?

Dorothy, the Cowardly Lion and the Winkies find the remains of the Tin Woodman and the Scarecrow and bring them back to life.

2. The Worldview Story Component: What is the essential tactic of the characters—that is, what above-the-surface macro behaviors are they employing that are linked to a universal human value?

Dorothy gets the Winkies on her side and reasons her way into recreating life.

3. The Heroic Journey 2.0 Component: What beyond-the-surface universal human values have changed for one or more characters in the scene? Which one of those value changes is most important and should be included in the Story Grid Spreadsheet?

When in doubt, the Story Grid rule of thumb is to highlight the value that best aligns with the progress of the global human value at stake in the story. *The Wonderful Wizard of Oz* is an Action Story, which has a global value at stake of Life/Death. Throughout the Story Grid Spreadsheet, we'll track the ways life is threatened or enhanced scene by scene.

The value shift for the Scarecrow and Tin Woodman is clear. *Death to Life.*

4. The Scene Event Synthesis: What Story Event sums up the scene's on-the-surface actions, essential above-the-surface worldview behavioral tactics, and beyond-the-surface value change? We will enter that event in the Story Grid Spreadsheet.

Dorothy brings her friends back to life with the help of the Cowardly Lion and the Winkies.

HOW THE SCENE ABIDES BY THE FIVE COMMANDMENTS OF STORYTELLING

Inciting Incident: The Cowardly Lion wishes the Tin Woodman and Scarecrow were with Dorothy and him.

Turning Point Progressive Complication: The Tin Woodman is in need of a complete overhaul and the Scarecrow's clothes are stuck in a high tree that cannot be climbed.

Crisis: Best bad choice. The longer Dorothy spends rescuing her friends, the longer she'll be away from her real home.

Climax: Dorothy chooses to stay away from Kansas until she can do everything she can for her friends.

Resolution: With the gang back intact, they decide to leave the Winkies and head back to collect their promise from Oz.

14

THE WINGED MONKEYS

SCENE 14

You will remember there was no road—not even a pathway— between the castle of the Wicked Witch and the Emerald City. *(Use of second person increases the narrative distance between the reader and the third person omniscient narrator)* When **the four travelers** went in search of **the Witch** she had seen them coming, and so sent **the Winged Monkeys** to bring them to her. It was much harder to find their way back through the big fields of buttercups and yellow daisies than it was being carried. They knew, of course, they must go straight east, toward the rising sun; and they started off in the right way. But at noon, when the sun was over their heads, they did not know which was east and which was west, and that was the reason they were lost in the great fields. They kept on walking, however, and at night the moon came out and shone brightly. So they lay down among the sweet smelling yellow flowers and slept soundly until morning—all but **the Scarecrow** and the **Tin Woodman.**

The next morning the sun was behind a cloud, but they started on, as if they were quite sure which way they were going.

"If we walk far enough," said **Dorothy**, "I am sure we shall sometime come to some place."

But **day by day** passed away, and they still saw nothing before them but the scarlet fields. The Scarecrow began to grumble a bit.

"We have surely lost our way," he said, "and unless we find it again in time to reach the Emerald City, I shall never get my brains."

"Nor I my heart," declared the Tin Woodman. "It seems to me I can scarcely wait till I get to Oz, and you must admit this is a very long journey."

"You see," said **the Cowardly Lion**, with a whimper, "I haven't the courage to keep tramping forever, without getting anywhere at all."

Then Dorothy lost heart. She sat down on the grass and looked at her companions, and they sat down and looked at her, and **Toto** found that for the first time in his life he was too tired to chase a butterfly that flew past his head. So he put out his tongue and panted and looked at Dorothy as if to ask what they should do next.

"Suppose we call the field mice," she suggested. "They could probably tell us the way to the Emerald City."

"To be sure they could," cried the Scarecrow. "Why didn't we think of that before?"

Dorothy blew the little whistle she had always carried about her neck since the Queen of the Mice had given it to her. In a few minutes they heard the pattering of tiny feet, and many of the small gray mice came running up to her. Among them was the Queen herself, who asked, in her squeaky little voice:

"What can I do for my friends?"

"We have lost our way," said Dorothy. "Can you tell us where the Emerald City is?"

"Certainly," answered the Queen; "but it is a great way off, for you have had it at your backs all this time." Then she noticed Dorothy's Golden Cap, and said, **"Why don't you use the charm of the Cap, and call the Winged Monkeys to you? They will carry you to the City of Oz in less than an hour."**

"I didn't know there was a charm," answered Dorothy, in surprise. "What is it?"

"It is written inside the Golden Cap," replied the Queen of the Mice. "But if you are going to call the Winged Monkeys we must run away, for they are full of mischief and think it great fun to plague us."

"Won't they hurt me?" asked the girl anxiously.

"Oh, no. They must obey the wearer of the Cap. Good-bye!" And she scampered out of sight, with all the mice hurrying after her.

Dorothy looked inside the Golden Cap and saw some words written upon the lining. These, she thought, must be the charm, so she read the directions carefully and put the Cap upon her head.

"Ep-pe, pep-pe, kak-ke!" she said, standing on her left foot.

"What did you say?" asked the Scarecrow, who did not know what she was doing.

"Hil-lo, hol-lo, hel-lo!" Dorothy went on, standing this time on her right foot.

"Hello!" replied the Tin Woodman calmly.

"Ziz-zy, zuz-zy, zik!" said Dorothy, who was now standing on both feet. This ended the saying of the charm, and they heard a great chattering and flapping of wings, as the band of Winged Monkeys flew up to them.

The King bowed low before Dorothy, and asked, "What is your command?"

"We wish to go to the Emerald City," said the child, "and we have lost our way."

"We will carry you," replied the King, and no sooner had he spoken than two of the Monkeys caught Dorothy in their arms and flew away with her. Others took the Scarecrow and the Woodman and the Lion, and one little Monkey seized Toto and flew after them, although the dog tried hard to bite him.

The Scarecrow and the Tin Woodman were rather frightened at first, for they remembered how badly the Winged Monkeys had treated them before; but they saw that no harm was intended, so they rode through the air quite cheerfully, and had a fine time looking at the pretty gardens and woods far below them.

Dorothy found herself riding easily between two of the biggest Monkeys, one of them the King himself. They had made a chair of their hands and were careful not to hurt her.

"Why do you have to obey the charm of the Golden Cap?" she asked.

"That is a long story," answered the King, with a winged laugh; "but as we have a long journey before us, I will pass the time by telling you about it, if you wish."

"I shall be glad to hear it," she replied.

"Once," began the leader, "we were a free people, living happily in the great forest, flying from tree to tree, eating nuts and fruit, and doing just as we pleased without calling anybody master. Perhaps some of us were rather too full of mischief at times, flying down to pull the tails of the animals that had no wings, chasing birds, and throwing nuts at the people who walked in the forest. But we were careless and happy and full of fun, and enjoyed every minute of the day. This was many years ago, long before **Oz came out of the clouds to rule over this land.**

"There lived here then, away at the North, **a beautiful princess,** who was also a powerful sorceress. All her magic was used to help the people, and she was never known to hurt anyone who was good. Her name was **Gayelette**, and she lived in a handsome palace built from great blocks of ruby. Everyone loved her, but her greatest sorrow was that she could find no one to love in return, since all the men were much too stupid and ugly to mate with one so beautiful and wise. At last, however, she found a boy who was handsome and manly and wise beyond his years. Gayelette made up her mind that when he grew to be a man she would make him her husband, so she took him to her ruby palace and used all her magic powers to make him as strong and good and lovely as any woman could wish. When he grew to manhood, **Quelala**, as he was called, was said to be the best and wisest man in all the land, while his manly beauty was so great that Gayelette loved him dearly, and hastened to make everything ready for the wedding.

"**My grandfather** was at that time the King of the Winged Monkeys which lived in the forest near Gayelette's palace, and the old fellow loved a joke better than a good dinner. One day, just before the wedding, my grandfather was flying out with his band when he saw Quelala walking beside the river. He was dressed in a rich costume of pink silk and purple velvet, and my grandfather thought he would see what he could do. At his word the band flew down and seized Quelala, carried him in their arms until they were over the middle of the river, and then dropped him into the water.

"'Swim out, my fine fellow,' cried my grandfather, 'and see if the water has spotted your clothes.' Quelala was much too wise not to swim, and he was not in the least spoiled by all his good fortune. He laughed, when he came to the top of the water, and swam in to shore. But when Gayelette came running out to him she found his silks and velvet all ruined by the river.

"The princess was angry, and she knew, of course, who did it. She had all the Winged Monkeys brought before her, and she said at first that their wings should be tied and they should be treated as they had treated Quelala, and dropped in the river. But my grandfather pleaded hard, for he knew the Monkeys would drown in the river with their wings tied, and Quelala said a kind word for them also; so that Gayelette finally spared them, on condition that the Winged Monkeys should ever after do **three times the bidding of the owner of the Golden Cap.** This Cap had been made for a wedding present to Quelala, and it is said to have cost the princess half her kingdom. Of course my grandfather and all the other Monkeys at once agreed to the condition, and that is how it happens that we are three times the slaves of the owner of the Golden Cap, whosoever he may be."

"And what became of them?" asked Dorothy, who had been greatly interested in the story.

"Quelala being the first owner of the Golden Cap," replied the Monkey, "he was the first to lay his wishes upon us. As his bride could not bear the sight of us, he called us all to him in the forest after he had married her and ordered us always to keep where she could never again set eyes on a Winged Monkey, which we were glad to do, for we were all afraid of her.

"This was all we ever had to do until the Golden Cap fell into the hands of the Wicked Witch of the West, **who made us enslave the Winkies, and afterward drive Oz himself out of the Land of the West.** Now the Golden Cap is yours, and three times you have the right to lay your wishes upon us."

As the Monkey King finished his story Dorothy looked down and saw the green, shining walls of the Emerald City before them. She wondered at the rapid flight of the Monkeys, but was glad the journey was over. The strange creatures set the travelers down carefully before the gate of the City, the King bowed low to Dorothy, and then flew swiftly away, followed by all his band.

"That was a good ride," said the little girl.

"Yes, and a quick way out of our troubles," replied the Lion. "How lucky it was you brought away that wonderful Cap!"

• ANALYZING THE SCENE •

STORY EVENT

A Story Event is an active change of a universal human value for one or more characters as a result of conflict (one character's desires clash with another's, or an environmental shift changes the universal human value).

A Working Scene contains at least one Story Event. To determine a scene's Story Event, answer these four Socratic questions:

1. The Action Story Component: What are the characters literally doing—that is, what are their micro on-the-surface actions?

Walking back to the Emerald City, the group gets lost.

2. The Worldview Story Component: What is the essential tactic of the characters—that is, what above-the-surface macro behaviors are they employing that are linked to a universal human value?

They are following their instincts about heading east and back to the Emerald City, but they then lose faith until they reason out a solution.

3. The Heroic Journey 2.0 Component: What beyond-the-surface universal human values have changed for one or more characters in the scene? Which one of those value changes is most important and should be included in the Story Grid Spreadsheet?

When in doubt, the Story Grid rule of thumb is to highlight the value that best aligns with the progress of the global human value at stake in the story. *The Wonderful Wizard of Oz* is an Action Story, which has a global value at stake of Life/Death. Throughout the Story Grid Spreadsheet, we'll track the ways life is threatened or enhanced scene by scene.

The value shift is clear for Dorothy and her companions, *Lost to Found*.

4. The Scene Event Synthesis: What Story Event sums up the scene's on-the-surface actions, essential above-the-surface worldview behavioral tactics, and beyond-the-surface value change? We will enter that event in the Story Grid Spreadsheet.

Dorothy uses the first of three cap wishes to get a ride to the Emerald City from the Winged Monkeys.

HOW THE SCENE ABIDES BY THE FIVE COMMANDMENTS OF STORYTELLING

Inciting Incident: The four travelers set out for the Emerald City.

Turning Point Progressive Complication: The queen of the field mice tells them about the magical cap and the connection to the Winged Monkeys.

Crisis: Best bad choice. Trusting the Winged Monkeys is dangerous as they were the ones who took them to the Wicked Witch of the West's castle. Not trusting them will keep them lost.

Climax: Dorothy calls in her first wish.

Resolution: The Monkeys take them to the Emerald City.

15

THE DISCOVERY OF OZ, THE TERRIBLE

SCENE 15

The four travelers walked up to the great gate of Emerald City and rang the bell. After ringing several times, it was opened by **the same Guardian of the Gates** they had met before.

"What! are you back again?" he asked, in surprise.

"Do you not see us?" answered **the Scarecrow**.

"But I thought you had gone to visit **the Wicked Witch of the West.**"

"We did visit her," said the Scarecrow.

"And she let you go again?" asked the man, in wonder.

"She could not help it, for she is melted," explained the Scarecrow.

"Melted! Well, that is good news, indeed," said the man. "Who melted her?"

"It was **Dorothy**," said **the Lion** gravely.

"Good gracious!" exclaimed the man, and he bowed very low indeed before her.

Then he led them into his little room and **locked the spectacles from the great box on all their eyes**, just as he had done before. Afterward they passed on through the gate into the Emerald City. When the people heard from the Guardian of the Gates that Dorothy had melted the Wicked Witch of the West, they all gathered around the travelers and followed them in a great crowd to the Palace of **Oz**.

The soldier with the green whiskers was still on guard before the door, but he let them in at once, and they were again met by **the beautiful green girl**, who showed each of them to their old rooms at once, so they might rest until the Great Oz was ready to receive them.

The soldier had the news carried straight to Oz that Dorothy and the other travelers had come back again, after destroying the Wicked Witch; but Oz made no reply. They thought the Great Wizard would send for them at once, but he did not. **They had no word from him the next day, nor the next, nor the next.** The waiting was tiresome and wearing, and at last they grew vexed that Oz should treat them in so poor a fashion, after sending them to undergo hardships and slavery. So the Scarecrow at last asked the green girl to take another message to Oz, saying if he did not let them in to see him at once they would call **the Winged Monkeys** to help them, and find out whether he kept his promises or not. When the Wizard was given this message he was so frightened that he sent word for them to come to the Throne Room at **four minutes after nine o'clock the next morning.** He had once met the Winged Monkeys in the Land of the West, and he did not wish to meet them again.

The four travelers passed a sleepless night, each thinking of the gift Oz had promised to bestow on him. Dorothy fell asleep only once, and then she dreamed she was in Kansas, where **Aunt Em** was telling her how glad she was to have her little girl at home again.

Promptly at nine o'clock the next morning the green-whiskered soldier came to them, and four minutes later they all went into **the Throne Room** of the Great Oz.

Of course each one of them expected to see the Wizard in the shape he had taken before, and all were greatly surprised when they looked about and saw no one at all in the room. They kept close to the door and closer to one another, for the stillness of the empty room was more dreadful than any of the forms they had seen Oz take.

Presently they heard a solemn Voice, that seemed to come from somewhere near the top of the great dome, and it said:

"I am Oz, the Great and Terrible. Why do you seek me?"

They looked again in every part of the room, and then, seeing no one, Dorothy asked, "Where are you?"

"I am everywhere," answered the Voice, "but to the eyes of common mortals I am invisible. I will now seat myself upon my throne, that you may converse with me." Indeed, the Voice seemed just then to come straight from the throne itself; so they walked toward it and stood in a row while Dorothy said:

"We have come to claim our promise, O Oz."

"What promise?" asked Oz.

"You promised to send me back to Kansas when the Wicked Witch was destroyed," said the girl.

"And you promised to give me brains," said the Scarecrow.

"And you promised to give me a heart," said the Tin Woodman.

"And you promised to give me courage," said the Cowardly Lion.

"Is the Wicked Witch really destroyed?" asked the Voice, and Dorothy thought it trembled a little.

"Yes," she answered, "I melted her with a bucket of water."

"Dear me," said the Voice, "how sudden! Well, come to me tomorrow, for I must have time to think it over."

"You've had plenty of time already," said the Tin Woodman angrily.

"We shan't wait a day longer," said the Scarecrow.

"You must keep your promises to us!" exclaimed Dorothy.

The Lion thought it might be as well to frighten the Wizard, so he gave a large, loud roar, which was so fierce and dreadful that **Toto** jumped away from him in alarm and tipped over the screen that stood in a corner. As it fell with a crash they looked that way, and the next moment all of them were filled with wonder. For they saw, standing in just the spot the screen had hidden, **a little old man**, with a bald head and a wrinkled face, who seemed to be as much surprised as they were. The Tin Woodman, raising his axe, rushed toward the little man and cried out, "Who are you?"

"I am Oz, the Great and Terrible," said the little man, in a trembling voice. "But don't strike me—please don't—and I'll do anything you want me to."

Our friends looked at him in surprise and dismay.

"I thought Oz was a great Head," said Dorothy.

"And I thought Oz was a lovely Lady," said the Scarecrow.

"And I thought Oz was a terrible Beast," said the Tin Woodman.

"And I thought Oz was a Ball of Fire," exclaimed the Lion.

"No, you are all wrong," said the little man meekly. "I have been making believe."

"Making believe!" cried Dorothy. "Are you not a Great Wizard?"

"Hush, my dear," he said. "Don't speak so loud, or you will be overheard—and I should be ruined. I'm supposed to be a Great Wizard."

"And aren't you?" she asked.

"Not a bit of it, my dear; I'm just a common man."

"You're more than that," said the Scarecrow, in a grieved tone; "you're a humbug."

"Exactly so!" declared the little man, rubbing his hands together as if it pleased him. "I am a humbug."

"But this is terrible," said the Tin Woodman. "How shall I ever get my heart?"

"Or I my courage?" asked the Lion.

"Or I my brains?" wailed the Scarecrow, wiping the tears from his eyes with his coat sleeve.

"My dear friends," said Oz, "I pray you not to speak of these little things. Think of me, and the terrible trouble I'm in at being found out."

"Doesn't anyone else know you're a humbug?" asked Dorothy.

"No one knows it but you four—and myself," replied Oz. "I have fooled everyone so long that I thought I should never be found out. It was a great mistake my ever letting you into the Throne Room. Usually I will not see even my subjects, and so they believe I am something terrible."

"But, I don't understand," said Dorothy, in bewilderment. "How was it that you appeared to me as a great Head?"

"That was one of my tricks," answered Oz. "Step this way, please, and I will tell you all about it."

He led the way to a small chamber in the rear of the Throne Room, and they all followed him. He pointed to one corner, in which lay the great Head, made out of many thicknesses of paper, and with a carefully painted face.

"This I hung from the ceiling by a wire," said Oz. "I stood behind the screen and pulled a thread, to make the eyes move and the mouth open."

"But how about the voice?" she inquired.

"Oh, I am a ventriloquist," said the little man. "I can throw the sound of my voice wherever I wish, so that you thought it was coming out of the Head. Here are the other things I used to deceive you." He showed the Scarecrow the dress and the mask he had worn when he seemed to be the lovely Lady. And the Tin Woodman saw that his terrible Beast was nothing but a lot of skins, sewn together, with slats to keep their sides out. As for the Ball of Fire, the false Wizard had hung that also from the ceiling. It was really a ball of cotton, but when oil was poured upon it the ball burned fiercely.

"Really," said the Scarecrow, "you ought to be ashamed of yourself for being such a humbug."

"I am—I certainly am," answered the little man sorrowfully; "but it was the only thing I could do. Sit down, please, there are plenty of chairs; and **I will tell you my story**."

So they sat down and listened while he told the following tale.

"I was born in Omaha—"

"Why, that isn't very far from Kansas!" cried Dorothy.

"No, but it's farther from here," he said, shaking his head at her sadly. "When I grew up I became a ventriloquist, and at that I was very well trained by a great master. I can imitate any kind of a bird or beast." Here he mewed so like a kitten that Toto pricked up his ears and looked everywhere to see where she was. "After a time," continued Oz, "I tired of that, and became a balloonist."

"What is that?" asked Dorothy.

"A man who goes up in a balloon on circus day, so as to draw a crowd of people together and get them to pay to see the circus," he explained.

"Oh," she said, "I know."

"Well, one day I went up in a balloon and the ropes got twisted, so that I couldn't come down again. It went way up above the clouds, so far that a current of air struck it and carried it many, many miles away. For a day and a night I traveled through the air, and on the morning of the second day I awoke and found the balloon floating over a strange and beautiful country.

"It came down gradually, and I was not hurt a bit. But I found myself in the midst of **a strange people**, who, seeing me come from the clouds, thought I was a great Wizard. Of course I let them think so, because they were afraid of me, and promised to do anything I wished them to.

"Just to amuse myself, and keep the good people busy, I ordered them to build this City, and my Palace; and they did it all willingly and well. Then I thought, as the country was so green and beautiful, I would call it the Emerald City; and to make the name fit better I put green spectacles on all the people, so that everything they saw was green."

"But isn't everything here green?" asked Dorothy.

"No more than in any other city," replied Oz; "but when you wear green spectacles, why of course everything you see looks green to you. The Emerald City was built a great many years ago, for I was a young man when the balloon brought me here, and I am a very old man now. But my people have worn green glasses on their eyes so long that most of them think it really is an Emerald City, and it certainly is a beautiful place, abounding in jewels and precious metals, and every good thing that is needed to make one happy. I have been good to the people, and they like me; but ever since this Palace was built, I have shut myself up and would not see any of them.

"One of my greatest fears was the Witches, for while I had no magical powers at all I soon found out that the Witches were really able to do wonderful things. There were four of them in this country, and they ruled the people who live in the North and South and East and West. Fortunately, the Witches of the North and South were good, and I knew they would do me no harm; but the Witches of the East and West were terribly wicked, and had they not thought I was more powerful than they themselves, they would surely have destroyed me. As it was, I lived in deadly fear of them for many years; so you can imagine how pleased I was when I heard your house had fallen on the Wicked Witch of the East. When you came to me, I was willing to promise anything if you would only do away with the other Witch; but, now that you have melted her, I am ashamed to say that I cannot keep my promises."

"I think you are a very bad man," said Dorothy.

"Oh, no, my dear; I'm really a very good man, but I'm a very bad Wizard, I must admit."

"Can't you give me brains?" asked the Scarecrow.

"You don't need them. You are learning something every day. A baby has brains, but it doesn't know much. Experience is the only thing that brings knowledge, and the longer you are on earth the more experience you are sure to get."

"That may all be true," said the Scarecrow, "but I shall be very unhappy unless you give me brains."

The false Wizard looked at him carefully.

"Well," he said with a sigh, "I'm not much of a magician, as I said; but if you will come to me tomorrow morning, I will stuff your head with brains. I cannot tell you how to use them, however; you must find that out for yourself."

"Oh, thank you—thank you!" cried the Scarecrow. "I'll find a way to use them, never fear!"

"But how about my courage?" asked the Lion anxiously.

"You have plenty of courage, I am sure," answered Oz. "All you need is confidence in yourself. There is no living thing that is not afraid when it faces danger. The True courage is in facing danger when you are afraid, and that kind of courage you have in plenty."

"Perhaps I have, but I'm scared just the same," said the Lion. "I shall really be very unhappy unless you give me the sort of courage that makes one forget he is afraid."

"Very well, I will give you that sort of courage tomorrow," replied Oz.

"How about my heart?" asked the Tin Woodman.

"Why, as for that," answered Oz, "I think you are wrong to want a heart. It makes most people unhappy. If you only knew it, you are in luck not to have a heart."

"That must be a matter of opinion," said the Tin Woodman. "For my part, I will bear all the unhappiness without a murmur, if you will give me the heart."

"Very well," answered Oz meekly. "Come to me tomorrow and you shall have a heart. I have played Wizard for so many years that I may as well continue the part a little longer."

"And now," said Dorothy, "how am I to get back to Kansas?"

"We shall have to think about that," replied the little man. "Give me two or three days to consider the matter and I'll try to find a way to carry you over the desert. In the meantime you shall all be treated as my guests, and while you live in the Palace my people will wait upon you and obey your slightest wish. There is only one thing I ask in return for my help—such as it is. You must keep my secret and tell no one I am a humbug."

They agreed to say nothing of what they had learned, and went back to their rooms in high spirits. Even Dorothy had hope that "The Great and Terrible Humbug," as she called him, would find a way to send her back to Kansas, and if he did she was willing to forgive him everything.

• ANALYZING THE SCENE •

STORY EVENT

A Story Event is an active change of a universal human value for one or more characters as a result of conflict (one character's desires clash with another's, or an environmental shift changes the universal human value).

A Working Scene contains at least one Story Event. To determine a scene's Story Event, answer these four Socratic questions:

1. The Action Story Component: What are the characters literally doing—that is, what are their micro on-the-surface actions?

The group meets with Oz after having lived up to their part of the arrangement.

2. The Worldview Story Component: What is the essential tactic of the characters—that is, what above-the-surface macro behaviors are they employing that are linked to a universal human value?

The group is demanding satisfaction and truth.

3. The Heroic Journey 2.0 Component: What beyond-the-surface universal human values have changed for one or more characters in the scene? Which one of those value changes is most important and should be included in the Story Grid Spreadsheet?

The group arrives hopeful that Oz will deliver on his end of the deal, discovers he's not a wizard but an ordinary man, and loses hope with the revelation. They then find hope again when Oz agrees to figure out how to get them what they want.

When in doubt, the Story Grid rule of thumb is to highlight the value that best aligns with the progress of the global human value at stake in the story. *The Wonderful Wizard of Oz* is an Action Story, which has a global value at stake of Life/Death. Throughout the Story Grid

Spreadsheet, we'll track the ways life is threatened or enhanced scene by scene.

Hopeful to Hopeless to Hopeful

4. The Scene Event Synthesis: What Story Event sums up the scene's on-the-surface actions, essential above-the-surface worldview behavioral tactics, and beyond-the-surface value change? We will enter that event in the Story Grid Spreadsheet.

Dorothy and the group discover that Oz is a fraud but take heart after he tells them he'll figure out how to get them what they want regardless.

HOW THE SCENE ABIDES BY THE FIVE COMMANDMENTS OF STORYTELLING

Inciting Incident: The four travelers are put off by Oz.

Turning Point Progressive Complication: They discover Oz is not a wizard.

Crisis: Best bad choice. Not telling the people of Emerald City that Oz is a fraud keeps them under servitude to a false god. Telling them will destroy all chances of them getting what they want.

Climax: Dorothy and company keep quiet about Oz's secret.

Resolution: Oz endeavors to figure out a way to give them what they want.

16

THE MAGIC ART OF THE GREAT HUMBUG

SCENE 16

Next morning **the Scarecrow** said to his friends:

"Congratulate me. I am going to **Oz** to get my brains at last. When I return I shall be as other men are."

"I have always liked you as you were," said **Dorothy** simply.

"It is kind of you to like a Scarecrow," he replied. "But surely you will think more of me when you hear the splendid thoughts my new brain is going to turn out." Then he said good-bye to them all in a cheerful voice and went to the Throne Room, where he rapped upon the door.

"Come in," said Oz.

The Scarecrow went in and found the little man sitting down by the window, engaged in deep thought.

"I have come for my brains," remarked the Scarecrow, a little uneasily.

"Oh, yes; sit down in that chair, please," replied Oz. "You must excuse me for taking your head off, but I shall have to do it in order to put your brains in their proper place."

"That's all right," said the Scarecrow. "You are quite welcome to take my head off, as long as it will be a better one when you put it on again."

So the Wizard unfastened his head and emptied out the straw. Then he entered the back room and took up a measure of bran, which he mixed with a great many pins and needles. Having shaken them together thoroughly, he filled the top of the Scarecrow's head with the mixture and stuffed the rest of the space with straw, to hold it in place.

When he had fastened the Scarecrow's head on his body again he said to him, "Hereafter you will be a great man, for I have given you a lot of bran-new brains."

The Scarecrow was both pleased and proud at the fulfillment of his greatest wish, and having thanked Oz warmly he went back to his friends.

Dorothy looked at him curiously. His head was quite bulged out at the top with brains.

"How do you feel?" she asked.

"I feel wise indeed," he answered earnestly. "When I get used to my brains I shall know everything."

"Why are those needles and pins sticking out of your head?" asked **the Tin Woodman.**

"That is proof that he is sharp," remarked **the Lion.**

"Well, I must go to Oz and get my heart," said the Woodman. So he walked to the Throne Room and knocked at the door.

"Come in," called Oz, and the Woodman entered and said, "I have come for my heart."

"Very well," answered the little man. "But I shall have to cut a hole in your breast, so I can put your heart in the right place. I hope it won't hurt you."

"Oh, no," answered the Woodman. "I shall not feel it at all."

So Oz brought a pair of tinsmith's shears and cut a small, square hole in the left side of the Tin Woodman's breast. Then, going to a chest of drawers, he took out a pretty heart, made entirely of silk and stuffed with sawdust.

"Isn't it a beauty?" he asked.

"It is, indeed!" replied the Woodman, who was greatly pleased. "But is it a kind heart?"

"Oh, very!" answered Oz. He put the heart in the Woodman's breast and then replaced the square of tin, soldering it neatly together where it had been cut.

"There," said he; "now you have a heart that any man might be proud of. I'm sorry I had to put a patch on your breast, but it really couldn't be helped."

"Never mind the patch," exclaimed the happy Woodman. "I am very grateful to you, and shall never forget your kindness."

"Don't speak of it," replied Oz.

Then the Tin Woodman went back to his friends, who wished him every joy on account of his good fortune.

The Lion now walked to the Throne Room and knocked at the door.

"Come in," said Oz.

"I have come for my courage," announced the Lion, entering the room.

"Very well," answered the little man; "I will get it for you."

He went to a cupboard and reaching up to a high shelf took down a square green bottle, the contents of which he poured into a green-gold dish, beautifully carved. Placing this before the Cowardly Lion, who sniffed at it as if he did not like it, the Wizard said:

"Drink."

"What is it?" asked the Lion.

"Well," answered Oz, "if it were inside of you, it would be courage. You know, of course, that courage is always inside one; so that this really cannot be called courage until you have swallowed it. Therefore I advise you to drink it as soon as possible."

The Lion hesitated no longer, but drank till the dish was empty.

"How do you feel now?" asked Oz.

"Full of courage," replied the Lion, who went joyfully back to his friends to tell them of his good fortune.

Oz, left to himself, smiled to think of his success in giving the Scarecrow and the Tin Woodman and the Lion exactly what they thought they wanted. "How can I help being a humbug," he said, "when all these people make me do things that everybody knows can't be done? It was easy to make the Scarecrow and the Lion and the

Woodman happy, because they imagined I could do anything. But it will take more than imagination to carry Dorothy back to Kansas, and I'm sure I don't know how it can be done."

STORY EVENT

A Story Event is an active change of a universal human value for one or more characters as a result of conflict (one character's desires clash with another's, or an environmental shift changes the universal human value).

A Working Scene contains at least one Story Event. To determine a scene's Story Event, answer these four Socratic questions:

1. The Action Story Component: What are the characters literally doing—that is, what are their micro on-the-surface actions?

The Scarecrow, the Tin Woodman and the Cowardly Lion get their placebo brains, heart and courage.

2. The Worldview Story Component: What is the essential tactic of the characters—that is, what above-the-surface macro behaviors are they employing that are linked to a universal human value?

Knowing that the three characters already possess what they're asking for, Oz humors the Scarecrow, Tin Woodman, and Lion with material objects that represent what they already possess.

3. The Heroic Journey 2.0 Component: What beyond-the-surface universal human values have changed for one or more characters in the scene? Which one of those value changes is most important and should be included in the Story Grid Spreadsheet?

When in doubt, the Story Grid rule of thumb is to highlight the value that best aligns with the progress of the global human value at stake in the story. *The Wonderful Wizard of Oz* is an Action Story, which has a global value at stake of Life/Death. Throughout the Story Grid Spreadsheet, we'll track the ways life is threatened or enhanced scene by scene.

The value shift is clear for the Scarecrow, Tin Woodman, and Lion, *Unsatisfied to Satisfied*.

4. The Scene Event Synthesis: What Story Event sums up the scene's on-the-surface actions, essential above-the-surface worldview behavioral tactics, and beyond-the-surface value change? We will enter that event in the Story Grid Spreadsheet.

The Scarecrow, the Tin Woodman and the Cowardly Lion find satisfaction.

HOW THE SCENE ABIDES BY THE FIVE COMMANDMENTS OF STORYTELLING

Inciting Incident: The time has come to meet with Oz for the Scarecrow, Tin Woodman, and Lion.

Turning Point Progressive Complication: The materials Oz uses to satisfy the Scarecrow, Tin Woodman, and Lion are material representations of their desires, not the actual objects desired.

Crisis: Best bad choice. If Oz points out that the materials he's using to satisfy the three characters are not real, the effect of the operations will not satisfy them. If he doesn't point out that the gifts are not real, the characters will believe a lie.

Climax: Oz promotes the lie.

Resolution: The three characters are satisfied.

17

HOW THE BALLOON WAS LAUNCHED

SCENE 17

For three days **Dorothy** heard nothing from **Oz**. These were sad days for the little girl, although her friends were all quite happy and contented. **The Scarecrow** told them there were wonderful thoughts in his head; but he would not say what they were because he knew no one could understand them but himself. When the **Tin Woodman** walked about he felt his heart rattling around in his breast; and he told Dorothy he had discovered it to be a kinder and more tender heart than the one he had owned when he was made of flesh. **The Lion** declared he was afraid of nothing on earth, and would gladly face an army or a dozen of the fierce Kalidahs.

Thus each of the little party was satisfied except Dorothy, who longed more than ever to get back to Kansas.

On the fourth day, to her great joy, Oz sent for her, and when she entered the Throne Room he greeted her pleasantly:

"Sit down, my dear; I think I have found the way to get you out of this country."

"And back to Kansas?" she asked eagerly.

"Well, I'm not sure about Kansas," said Oz, "for I haven't the faintest notion which way it lies. But the first thing to do is to cross the desert, and then it should be easy to find your way home."

"How can I cross the desert?" she inquired.

"Well, I'll tell you what I think," said the little man. "You see, when I came to this country it was in a balloon. You also came through the air, being carried by a cyclone. So I believe the best way to get across the desert will be through the air. Now, it is quite beyond my powers to make a cyclone; but I've been thinking the matter over, and I believe I can make a balloon."

"How?" asked Dorothy.

"A balloon," said Oz, "is made of silk, which is coated with glue to keep the gas in it. I have plenty of silk in the Palace, so it will be no trouble to make the balloon. But in all this country there is no gas to fill the balloon with, to make it float."

"If it won't float," remarked Dorothy, "it will be of no use to us."

"True," answered Oz. "But there is another way to make it float, which is to fill it with hot air. Hot air isn't as good as gas, for if the air should get cold the balloon would come down in the desert, and we should be lost."

"We!" exclaimed the girl. "Are you going with me?"

"Yes, of course," replied Oz. "I am tired of being such a humbug. If I should go out of this Palace my people would soon discover I am not a Wizard, and then they would be vexed with me for having deceived them. So I have to stay shut up in these rooms all day, and it gets tiresome. I'd much rather go back to Kansas with you and be in a circus again."

"I shall be glad to have your company," said Dorothy.

"Thank you," he answered. "Now, if you will help me sew the silk together, we will begin to work on our balloon."

So Dorothy took a needle and thread, and as fast as Oz cut the strips of silk into proper shape the girl sewed them neatly together. First there was a strip of light green silk, then a strip of dark green and then a strip of emerald green; for Oz had a fancy to make the balloon in different shades of the color about them. It took three days to sew all the strips together, but when it was finished they had a big bag of green silk more than twenty feet long.

Then Oz painted it on the inside with a coat of thin glue, to make it airtight, after which he announced that the balloon was ready.

"But we must have a basket to ride in," he said. So he sent the soldier with the green whiskers for a big clothes basket, which he fastened with many ropes to the bottom of the balloon.

When it was all ready, Oz sent word to his people that he was going to make a visit to a great brother Wizard who lived in the clouds. The news spread rapidly throughout the city and everyone came to see the wonderful sight.

Oz ordered the balloon carried out in front of the Palace, and the people gazed upon it with much curiosity. The Tin Woodman had chopped a big pile of wood, and now he made a fire of it, and Oz held the bottom of the balloon over the fire so that the hot air that arose from it would be caught in the silken bag. Gradually the balloon swelled out and rose into the air, until finally the basket just touched the ground.

Then Oz got into the basket and said to all the people in a loud voice:

"I am now going away to make a visit. While I am gone the Scarecrow will rule over you. I command you to obey him as you would me."

The balloon was by this time tugging hard at the rope that held it to the ground, for the air within it was hot, and this made it so much lighter in weight than the air without that it pulled hard to rise into the sky.

"Come, Dorothy!" cried the Wizard. "Hurry up, or the balloon will fly away."

"I can't find **Toto** anywhere," replied Dorothy, who did not wish to leave her little dog behind. Toto had run into the crowd to bark at a kitten, and Dorothy at last found him. She picked him up and ran towards the balloon.

She was within a few steps of it, and Oz was holding out his hands to help her into the basket, when, crack! went the ropes, and the balloon rose into the air without her.

"Come back!" she screamed. "I want to go, too!"

"I can't come back, my dear," called Oz from the basket. "Good-bye!"

"Good-bye!" shouted everyone, and all eyes were turned upward to where the Wizard was riding in the basket, rising every moment farther and farther into the sky.

And that was the last any of them ever saw of Oz, the Wonderful Wizard, though he may have reached Omaha safely, and be there now, for all we know. But the people remembered him lovingly, and said to one another:

"Oz was always our friend. When he was here he built for us this beautiful Emerald City, and now he is gone he has left the Wise Scarecrow to rule over us."

Still, for many days they grieved over the loss of the Wonderful Wizard, and would not be comforted.

STORY EVENT

A Story Event is an active change of a universal human value for one or more characters as a result of conflict (one character's desires clash with another's, or an environmental shift changes the universal human value).

A Working Scene contains at least one Story Event. To determine a scene's Story Event, answer these four Socratic questions:

1. The Action Story Component: What are the characters literally doing—that is, what are their micro on-the-surface actions?

Dorothy and Oz make a balloon to escape over the desert between the Emerald City and home.

2. The Worldview Story Component: What is the essential tactic of the characters—that is, what above-the-surface macro behaviors are they employing that are linked to a universal human value?

Dorothy and Oz are shaping their dreams of returning home into reality.

3. The Heroic Journey 2.0 Component: What beyond-the-surface universal human values have changed for one or more characters in the scene? Which one of those value changes is most important and should be included in the Story Grid Spreadsheet?

When in doubt, the Story Grid rule of thumb is to highlight the value that best aligns with the progress of the global human value at stake in the story. *The Wonderful Wizard of Oz* is an Action Story, which has a global value at stake of Life/Death. Throughout the Story Grid Spreadsheet, we'll track the ways life is threatened or enhanced scene by scene.

The value shift for Dorothy is clear, *Hope to All Is Lost*.

4. The Scene Event Synthesis: What Story Event sums up the scene's on-the-surface actions, essential above-the-surface worldview behavioral tactics, and beyond-the-surface value change? We will enter that event in the Story Grid Spreadsheet.

Oz puts in motion his plan to leave via hot air balloon with Dorothy but leaves without her.

HOW THE SCENE ABIDES BY THE FIVE COMMANDMENTS OF STORYTELLING

Inciting Incident: Oz figures out how to leave.

Turning Point Progressive Complication: Toto escapes.

Crisis: Best bad choice. If Dorothy abandons Toto to find her way home, she'll condemn him to living in the Emerald City for the rest of his life.

Climax: Dorothy stays to find Toto.

Resolution: Oz leaves, but Dorothy stays.

18

AWAY TO THE SOUTH

SCENE 18

Dorothy wept bitterly at the passing of her hope to get home to Kansas again; but when she thought it all over she was glad she had not gone up in a balloon. And she also felt sorry at losing **Oz**, and so did her companions.

The Tin Woodman came to her and said:

"Truly I should be ungrateful if I failed to mourn for the man who gave me my lovely heart. I should like to cry a little because Oz is gone, if you will kindly wipe away my tears, so that I shall not rust."

"With pleasure," she answered, and brought a towel at once. Then the Tin Woodman wept for several minutes, and she watched the tears carefully and wiped them away with the towel. When he had finished, he thanked her kindly and oiled himself thoroughly with his jeweled oil-can, to guard against mishap.

The Scarecrow was now the ruler of the Emerald City, and although he was not a Wizard the people were proud of him. "For," they said, "there is not another city in all the world that is ruled by a stuffed man." And, so far as they knew, they were quite right.

The morning after the balloon had gone up with Oz, the four travelers met in the Throne Room and talked matters over. The

Scarecrow sat in the big throne and the others stood respectfully before him.

"We are not so unlucky," said the new ruler, "for this Palace and the Emerald City belong to us, and we can do just as we please. When I remember that a short time ago I was up on a pole in a farmer's cornfield, and that now I am the ruler of this beautiful City, I am quite satisfied with my lot."

"I also," said the Tin Woodman, "am well-pleased with my new heart; and, really, that was the only thing I wished in all the world."

"For my part, I am content in knowing I am as brave as any beast that ever lived, if not braver," said the Lion modestly.

"If Dorothy would only be contented to live in the Emerald City," continued the Scarecrow, "we might all be happy together."

"But I don't want to live here," cried Dorothy. "I want to go to Kansas, and live with **Aunt Em** and **Uncle Henry**."

"Well, then, what can be done?" inquired the Woodman.

The Scarecrow decided to think, and he thought so hard that the pins and needles began to stick out of his brains. Finally he said:

"Why not call **the Winged Monkeys**, and ask them to carry you over the desert?"

"I never thought of that!" said Dorothy joyfully. "It's just the thing. I'll go at once for the Golden Cap."

When she brought it into the Throne Room she spoke the magic words, and soon the band of Winged Monkeys flew in through the open window and stood beside her.

"This is the second time you have called us," said **the Monkey King**, bowing before the little girl. "What do you wish?"

"I want you to fly with me to Kansas," said Dorothy.

But **the Monkey King** shook his head.

"That cannot be done," he said. "We belong to this country alone, and cannot leave it. There has never been a Winged Monkey in Kansas yet, and I suppose there never will be, for they don't belong there. We shall be glad to serve you in any way in our power, but we cannot cross the desert. Good-bye."

And with another bow, the Monkey King spread his wings and flew away through the window, followed by all his band.

Dorothy was ready to cry with disappointment. "I have wasted the charm of the Golden Cap to no purpose," she said, "for the Winged Monkeys cannot help me."

"It is certainly too bad!" said the tender-hearted Woodman.

The Scarecrow was thinking again, and his head bulged out so horribly that Dorothy feared it would burst.

"Let us call in **the soldier with the green whiskers**," he said, "and ask his advice."

So the soldier was summoned and entered the Throne Room timidly, for while Oz was alive he never was allowed to come farther than the door.

"This little girl," said the Scarecrow to the soldier, "wishes to cross the desert. How can she do so?"

"I cannot tell," answered the soldier, "for nobody has ever crossed the desert, unless it is Oz himself."

"Is there no one who can help me?" asked Dorothy earnestly.

"Glinda might," he suggested.

"Who is Glinda?" inquired the Scarecrow.

"The Witch of the South. She is the most powerful of all the Witches, and rules over the Quadlings. Besides, her castle stands on the edge of the desert, so she may know a way to cross it."

"Glinda is a Good Witch, isn't she?" asked the child.

"The Quadlings think she is good," said the soldier, "and she is kind to everyone. I have heard that Glinda is a beautiful woman, who knows how to keep young in spite of the many years she has lived."

"How can I get to her castle?" asked Dorothy.

"The road is straight to the South," he answered, "but it is said to be full of dangers to travelers. There are **wild beasts in the woods**, and **a race of queer men** who do not like strangers to cross their country. For this reason none of the Quadlings ever come to the Emerald City."

The soldier then left them and the Scarecrow said:

"It seems, in spite of dangers, that the best thing Dorothy can do is to travel to the Land of the South and ask Glinda to help her. For, of course, if Dorothy stays here she will never get back to Kansas."

"You must have been thinking again," remarked the Tin Woodman.

"I have," said the Scarecrow.

"I shall go with Dorothy," declared **the Lion**, "for I am tired of your city and long for the woods and the country again. I am really a wild beast, you know. Besides, Dorothy will need someone to protect her."

"That is true," agreed the Woodman. "My axe may be of service to her; so I also will go with her to the Land of the South."

"When shall we start?" asked the Scarecrow.

"Are you going?" they asked, in surprise.

"Certainly. If it wasn't for Dorothy I should never have had brains. She lifted me from the pole in the cornfield and brought me to the Emerald City. So my good luck is all due to her, and I shall never leave her until she starts back to Kansas for good and all."

"Thank you," said Dorothy gratefully. "You are all very kind to me. But I should like to start as soon as possible."

"We shall go tomorrow morning," returned the Scarecrow. "So now let us all get ready, for it will be a long journey."

• ANALYZING THE SCENE •

STORY EVENT

A Story Event is an active change of a universal human value for one or more characters as a result of conflict (one character's desires clash with another's, or an environmental shift changes the universal human value).

A Working Scene contains at least one Story Event. To determine a scene's Story Event, answer these four Socratic questions:

1. The Action Story Component: What are the characters literally doing—that is, what are their micro on-the-surface actions?

Dorothy, the Scarecrow, the Tin Woodman and the Lion debate how to solve the "how to get back to Kansas" dilemma.

2. The Worldview Story Component: What is the essential tactic of the characters—that is, what above-the-surface macro behaviors are they employing that are linked to a universal human value?

The Scarecrow, the Tin Woodman, and the Lion are empathetically joining forces to help Dorothy solve her problem.

3. The Heroic Journey 2.0 Component: What beyond-the-surface universal human values have changed for one or more characters in the scene? Which one of those value changes is most important and should be included in the Story Grid Spreadsheet?

When in doubt, the Story Grid rule of thumb is to highlight the value that best aligns with the progress of the global human value at stake in the story. *The Wonderful Wizard of Oz* is an Action Story, which has a global value at stake of Life/Death. Throughout the Story Grid Spreadsheet, we'll track the ways life is threatened or enhanced scene by scene.

The value shift for Dorothy is clear, *Despair to Hope*.

4. The Scene Event Synthesis: What Story Event sums up the scene's on-the-surface actions, essential above-the-surface worldview behavioral tactics, and beyond-the-surface value change? We will enter that event in the Story Grid Spreadsheet.

After a series of dead-end ideas, the group resolves to seek the help of Glinda the Good Witch and plans to set off again to find her.

HOW THE SCENE ABIDES BY THE FIVE COMMANDMENTS OF STORYTELLING

Inciting Incident: Dorothy is stranded at the Emerald City.

Turning Point Progressive Complication: Glinda the good witch is someone worth seeking counsel.

Crisis: Best bad choice. If the team sets off to meet with Glinda the Good Witch, they'll have to confront beasts and queer men. If they don't Dorothy will never get home again.

Climax: The team agrees to leave the next morning.

Resolution: The team makes preparations for their journey.

19

ATTACKED BY THE FIGHTING TREES

SCENE 19

The next morning **Dorothy** kissed the **pretty green girl** good-bye, and they all shook hands with the **soldier with the green whiskers,** who had walked with them as far as the gate. When the **Guardian of the Gate** saw them again he wondered greatly that they could leave the beautiful City to get into new trouble. But he at once unlocked their spectacles, which he put back into the green box, and gave them many good wishes to carry with them.

"You are now our ruler," he said to **the Scarecrow;** "so you must come back to us as soon as possible."

"I certainly shall if I am able," the Scarecrow replied; "but I must help Dorothy to get home, first."

As Dorothy bade the good-natured Guardian a last farewell she said:

"I have been very kindly treated in your lovely City, and everyone has been good to me. I cannot tell you how grateful I am."

"Don't try, my dear," he answered. "We should like to keep you with us, but if it is your wish to return to Kansas, I hope you will find a way." He then opened the gate of the outer wall, and they walked forth and started upon their journey.

The sun shone brightly as our friends turned their faces toward the Land of the South. They were all in the best of spirits, and laughed and chatted together. Dorothy was once more filled with the hope of getting home, and the Scarecrow and **the Tin Woodman** were glad to be of use to her. As for **the Lion**, he sniffed the fresh air with delight and whisked his tail from side to side in pure joy at being in the country again, while **Toto** ran around them and chased the moths and butterflies, barking merrily all the time.

"City life does not agree with me at all," remarked the Lion, as they walked along at a brisk pace. "I have lost much flesh since I lived there, and now I am anxious for a chance to show the other beasts how courageous I have grown."

They now turned and took a last look at the Emerald City. All they could see was a mass of towers and steeples behind the green walls, and high up above everything the spires and dome of the Palace of Oz.

"**Oz** was not such a bad Wizard, after all," said the Tin Woodman, as he felt his heart rattling around in his breast.

"He knew how to give me brains, and very good brains, too," said the Scarecrow.

"If Oz had taken a dose of the same courage he gave me," added the Lion, "he would have been a brave man."

Dorothy said nothing. Oz had not kept the promise he made her, but he had done his best, so she forgave him. As he said, he was a good man, even if he was a bad Wizard.

The first day's journey was through the green fields and bright flowers that stretched about the Emerald City on every side. They slept that night on the grass, with nothing but the stars over them; and they rested very well indeed.

In the morning they traveled on until they came to a thick wood. There was no way of going around it, for it seemed to extend to the right and left as far as they could see; and, besides, they did not dare change the direction of their journey for fear of getting lost. So they looked for the place where it would be easiest to get into the forest.

The Scarecrow, who was in the lead, finally discovered a big tree with such wide-spreading branches that there was room for the party to pass underneath. So he walked forward to the tree, but just as he came under the first branches they bent down and twined around him, and the next minute he was raised from the ground and flung headlong among his fellow travelers.

This did not hurt the Scarecrow, but it surprised him, and he looked rather dizzy when Dorothy picked him up.

"Here is another space between the trees," called the Lion.

"Let me try it first," said the Scarecrow, "for it doesn't hurt me to get thrown about." He walked up to another tree, as he spoke, but its branches immediately seized him and tossed him back again.

"This is strange," exclaimed Dorothy. "What shall we do?"

"The trees seem to have made up their minds to fight us, and stop our journey," remarked the Lion.

"I believe I will try it myself," said the Woodman, and shouldering his axe, he marched up to the first tree that had handled the Scarecrow so roughly. When a big branch bent down to seize him the Woodman chopped at it so fiercely that he cut it in two. At once the tree began shaking all its branches as if in pain, and the Tin Woodman passed safely under it.

"Come on!" he shouted to the others. "Be quick!" They all ran forward and passed under the tree without injury, except Toto, who was caught by a small branch and shaken until he howled. But the Woodman promptly chopped off the branch and set the little dog free.

The other trees of the forest did nothing to keep them back, so they made up their minds that only the first row of trees could bend down their branches, and that probably these were the policemen of the forest, and given this wonderful power in order to keep strangers out of it.

The four travelers walked with ease through the trees until they came to the farther edge of the wood. Then, to their surprise, they found before them a high wall which seemed to be made of white china. It was smooth, like the surface of a dish, and higher than their heads.

"What shall we do now?" asked Dorothy.

"I will make a ladder," said the Tin Woodman, "for we certainly must climb over the wall."

STORY EVENT

A Story Event is an active change of a universal human value for one or more characters as a result of conflict (one character's desires clash with another's, or an environmental shift changes the universal human value).

A Working Scene contains at least one Story Event. To determine a scene's Story Event, answer these four Socratic questions:

1. The Action Story Component: What are the characters literally doing—that is, what are their micro on-the-surface actions?

Dorothy, the Scarecrow, the Tin Woodman and the Lion are back on the road on their way to see Glinda the Good Witch.

2. The Worldview Story Component: What is the essential tactic of the characters—that is, what above-the-surface macro behaviors are they employing that are linked to a universal human value?

The group is operating at peak efficiency as a collective with a sum greater than its individual parts.

3. The Heroic Journey 2.0 Component: What beyond-the-surface universal human values have changed for one or more characters in the scene? Which one of those value changes is most important and should be included in the Story Grid Spreadsheet?

When in doubt, the Story Grid rule of thumb is to highlight the value that best aligns with the progress of the global human value at stake in the story. *The Wonderful Wizard of Oz* is an Action Story, which has a global value at stake of Life/Death. Throughout the Story Grid Spreadsheet, we'll track the ways life is threatened or enhanced scene by scene.

The value shift is clear for Dorothy and her companions, *Stymied to Remedied*.

4. The Scene Event Synthesis: What Story Event sums up the scene's on-the-surface actions, essential above-the-surface worldview behavioral tactics, and beyond-the-surface value change? We will enter that event in the Story Grid Spreadsheet.

The group travels toward Glinda and must overcome guardian trees. They then face the hurdle of getting over a porcelain wall.

HOW THE SCENE ABIDES BY THE FIVE COMMANDMENTS OF STORYTELLING

Inciting Incident: Dorothy and her companions leave Emerald City.

Turning Point Progressive Complication: The group comes to a forest and is met by aggressive trees that will not allow them to enter.

Crisis: Best bad choice. If the team does not get through the forest, they will not meet Glinda. If they try to get into the forest, they will be possibly hurt.

Climax: The Tin Woodman cuts the arms of the trees that try to grab them and gets them into the forest's safe zone.

Resolution: The team comes to another obstacle after they've gone through the forest.

20

THE DAINTY CHINA COUNTRY

SCENE 20

While **the Woodman** was making a ladder from wood which he found in the forest **Dorothy** lay down and slept, for she was tired by the long walk. **The Lion** also curled himself up to sleep and **Toto** lay beside him.

The Scarecrow watched the Woodman while he worked, and said to him:

"I cannot think why this wall is here, nor what it is made of."

"Rest your brains and do not worry about the wall," replied the Woodman. "When we have climbed over it, we shall know what is on the other side."

After a time the ladder was finished. It looked clumsy, but the Tin Woodman was sure it was strong and would answer their purpose. The Scarecrow waked Dorothy and the Lion and Toto, and told them that the ladder was ready. The Scarecrow climbed up the ladder first, but he was so awkward that Dorothy had to follow close behind and keep him from falling off. When he got his head over the top of the wall the Scarecrow said, "Oh, my!"

"Go on," exclaimed Dorothy.

So the Scarecrow climbed farther up and sat down on the top of the wall, and Dorothy put her head over and cried, "Oh, my!" just as the Scarecrow had done.

Then Toto came up, and immediately began to bark, but Dorothy made him be still.

The Lion climbed the ladder next, and the Tin Woodman came last; but both of them cried, "Oh, my!" as soon as they looked over the wall. When they were all sitting in a row on the top of the wall, they looked down and saw a strange sight.

Before them was a great stretch of country having a floor as smooth and shining and white as the bottom of a big platter. Scattered around were many houses made entirely of china and painted in the brightest colors. These houses were quite small, the biggest of them reaching only as high as Dorothy's waist. There were also pretty little barns, with china fences around them; and many cows and sheep and horses and pigs and chickens, all made of china, were standing about in groups.

But the strangest of all were the people who lived in this queer country. There were **milkmaids and shepherdesses**, with brightly colored bodices and golden spots all over their gowns; and **princesses** with most gorgeous frocks of silver and gold and purple; and **shepherds** dressed in knee breeches with pink and yellow and blue stripes down them, and golden buckles on their shoes; **and princes** with jeweled crowns upon their heads, wearing ermine robes and satin doublets; and **funny clowns** in ruffled gowns, with round red spots upon their cheeks and tall, pointed caps. And, strangest of all, these people were all made of china, even to their clothes, and were so small that the tallest of them was no higher than Dorothy's knee.

No one did so much as look at the travelers at first, except one **little purple china dog** with an extra-large head, which came to the wall and barked at them in a tiny voice, afterwards running away again.

"How shall we get down?" asked Dorothy.

They found the ladder so heavy they could not pull it up, so the Scarecrow fell off the wall and the others jumped down upon him so that the hard floor would not hurt their feet. Of course they took pains not to light on his head and get the pins in their feet. When all were safely down they picked up the Scarecrow, whose body was quite flattened out, and patted his straw into shape again.

"We must cross this strange place in order to get to the other side," said Dorothy, "for it would be unwise for us to go any other way except due South."

They began walking through the country of the china people, and the first thing they came to was a **china milkmaid milking a china cow.** As they drew near, the cow suddenly gave a kick and kicked over the stool, the pail, and even the milkmaid herself, and all fell on the china ground with a great clatter.

Dorothy was shocked to see that the cow had broken her leg off, and that the pail was lying in several small pieces, while the poor milkmaid had a nick in her left elbow.

"There!" cried the milkmaid angrily. "See what you have done! My cow has broken her leg, and I must take her to the mender's shop and have it glued on again. What do you mean by coming here and frightening my cow?"

"I'm very sorry," returned Dorothy. "Please forgive us."

But the pretty milkmaid was much too vexed to make any answer. She picked up the leg sulkily and led her cow away, the poor animal limping on three legs. As she left them the milkmaid cast many reproachful glances over her shoulder at the clumsy strangers, holding her nicked elbow close to her side.

Dorothy was quite grieved at this mishap.

"We must be very careful here," said the kind-hearted Woodman, "or we may hurt these pretty little people so they will never get over it."

A little farther on Dorothy met **a most beautifully dressed young Princess,** who stopped short as she saw the strangers and started to run away.

Dorothy wanted to see more of the Princess, so she ran after her. But the china girl cried out:

"Don't chase me! Don't chase me!"

She had such a frightened little voice that Dorothy stopped and said, "Why not?"

"Because," answered the Princess, also stopping, a safe distance away, "if I run I may fall down and break myself."

"But could you not be mended?" asked the girl.

"Oh, yes; but one is never so pretty after being mended, you know," replied the Princess.

"I suppose not," said Dorothy.

"Now there is **Mr. Joker**, one of our clowns," continued the china lady, "who is always trying to stand upon his head. He has broken himself so often that he is mended in a hundred places, and doesn't look at all pretty. Here he comes now, so you can see for yourself."

Indeed, a jolly little clown came walking toward them, and Dorothy could see that in spite of his pretty clothes of red and yellow and green he was completely covered with cracks, running every which way and showing plainly that he had been mended in many places.

The Clown put his hands in his pockets, and after puffing out his cheeks and nodding his head at them saucily, he said:

"My lady fair,

Why do you stare

At poor old Mr. Joker?

You're quite as stiff

And prim as if

You'd eaten up a poker!"

"Be quiet, sir!" said the Princess. "Can't you see these are strangers, and should be treated with respect?"

"Well, that's respect, I expect," declared the Clown, and immediately stood upon his head.

"Don't mind Mr. Joker," said the Princess to Dorothy. "He is considerably cracked in his head, and that makes him foolish."

"Oh, I don't mind him a bit," said Dorothy. "But you are so beautiful," she continued, "that I am sure I could love you dearly. Won't you let me carry you back to Kansas, and stand you on Aunt Em's mantel? I could carry you in my basket."

"That would make me very unhappy," answered the china Princess. "You see, here in our country we live contentedly, and can talk and move around as we please. But whenever any of us are taken away our joints at once stiffen, and we can only stand straight and look pretty. Of course that is all that is expected of us when we are on mantels and cabinets and drawing-room tables, but our lives are much pleasanter here in our own country."

"I would not make you unhappy for all the world!" exclaimed Dorothy. "So I'll just say good-bye."

"Good-bye," replied the Princess.

They walked carefully through the china country. The little animals and all the people scampered out of their way, fearing the strangers would break them, and after an hour or so the travelers reached the other side of the country and came to another china wall.

It was not so high as the first, however, and by standing upon the Lion's back they all managed to scramble to the top. Then the Lion gathered his legs under him and jumped on the wall; but just as he jumped, he upset a china church with his tail and smashed it all to pieces.

"That was too bad," said Dorothy, "but really I think we were lucky in not doing these little people more harm than breaking a cow's leg and a church. They are all so brittle!"

"They are, indeed," said the Scarecrow, "and I am thankful I am made of straw and cannot be easily damaged. There are worse things in the world than being a Scarecrow."

STORY EVENT

A Story Event is an active change of a universal human value for one or more characters as a result of conflict (one character's desires clash with another's, or an environmental shift changes the universal human value).

A Working Scene contains at least one Story Event. To determine a scene's Story Event, answer these four Socratic questions:

1. The Action Story Component: What are the characters literally doing—that is, what are their micro on-the-surface actions?

The group proceeds into a magical world made up of beings made of china and accidentally causes damage.

2. The Worldview Story Component: What is the essential tactic of the characters—that is, what above-the-surface macro behaviors are they employing that are linked to a universal human value?

The group is doing their best to respect the environment and be gracious guests.

3. The Heroic Journey 2.0 Component: What beyond-the-surface universal human values have changed for one or more characters in the scene? Which one of those value changes is most important and should be included in the Story Grid Spreadsheet?

Despite the group's care, their presence causes damage to the china world.

When in doubt, the Story Grid rule of thumb is to highlight the value that best aligns with the progress of the global human value at stake in the story. *The Wonderful Wizard of Oz* is an Action Story, which has a global value at stake of Life/Death. Throughout the Story Grid

Spreadsheet, we'll track the ways life is threatened or enhanced scene by scene.

Innocent to Guilty

4. The Scene Event Synthesis: What Story Event sums up the scene's on-the-surface actions, essential above-the-surface worldview behavioral tactics, and beyond-the-surface value change? We will enter that event in the Story Grid Spreadsheet.

The group makes their way through a magical world filled with beings made of china and accidently disturbs it.

HOW THE SCENE ABIDES BY THE FIVE COMMANDMENTS OF STORYTELLING

Inciting Incident: Dorothy and the crew climb over a ladder into a china land.

Turning Point Progressive Complication: Dorothy frightens a china cow, and it breaks its leg.

Crisis: Irreconcilable Goods: If the team does not get through the china land, they will not meet Glinda. The longer they are there, the worse it is for the china citizens.

Climax: The crew presses forward on their own agenda.

Resolution: The china world is damaged.

21

THE LION BECOMES THE KING OF BEASTS

SCENE 21

After climbing down from the china wall the travelers found themselves in a disagreeable country, full of bogs and marshes and covered with tall, rank grass. It was difficult to walk without falling into muddy holes, for the grass was so thick that it hid them from sight. However, by carefully picking their way, they got safely along until they reached solid ground. But here the country seemed wilder than ever, and after a long and tiresome walk through the underbrush they entered another forest, where the trees were bigger and older than any they had ever seen.

"This forest is perfectly delightful," declared **the Lion**, looking around him with joy. "Never have I seen a more beautiful place."

"It seems gloomy," said **the Scarecrow.**

"Not a bit of it," answered the Lion. "I should like to live here all my life. See how soft the dried leaves are under your feet and how rich and green the moss is that clings to these old trees. Surely no wild beast could wish a pleasanter home."

"Perhaps there are wild beasts in the forest now," said **Dorothy.**

"I suppose there are," returned the Lion, "but I do not see any of them about."

They walked through the forest until it became too dark to go any farther. Dorothy and **Toto** and the Lion lay down to sleep, while **the Woodman** and the Scarecrow kept watch over them as usual.

When morning came, they started again. Before they had gone far they heard a low rumble, as of the growling of many wild animals. Toto whimpered a little, but none of the others was frightened, and they kept along the well-trodden path until they came to an opening in the wood, in which were gathered hundreds of beasts of every variety. There were tigers and elephants and bears and wolves and foxes and all the others in the natural history, and for a moment Dorothy was afraid. But the Lion explained that the animals were holding a meeting, and he judged by their snarling and growling that they were in great trouble.

As he spoke several of the beasts caught sight of him, and at once the great assemblage hushed as if by magic. The biggest of the tigers came up to the Lion and bowed, saying:

"Welcome, O King of Beasts! You have come in good time to fight our enemy and bring peace to all the animals of the forest once more."

"What is your trouble?" asked the Lion quietly.

"We are all threatened," answered the tiger, "by a fierce enemy which has lately come into this forest. It is a most tremendous monster, like a great spider, with a body as big as an elephant and legs as long as a tree trunk. It has eight of these long legs, and as the monster crawls through the forest he seizes an animal with a leg and drags it to his mouth, where he eats it as a spider does a fly. Not one of us is safe while this fierce creature is alive, and we had called a meeting to decide how to take care of ourselves when you came among us."

The Lion thought for a moment.

"Are there any other lions in this forest?" he asked.

"No; there were some, but the monster has eaten them all. And, besides, they were none of them nearly so large and brave as you."

"If I put an end to your enemy, will you bow down to me and obey me as King of the Forest?" inquired the Lion.

"We will do that gladly," returned the tiger; and all the other beasts roared with a mighty roar: "We will!"

"Where is this great spider of yours now?" asked the Lion.

"Yonder, among the oak trees," said the tiger, pointing with his forefoot.

"Take good care of these friends of mine," said the Lion, "and I will go at once to fight the monster."

He bade his comrades good-bye and marched proudly away to do battle with the enemy.

The great spider was lying asleep when the Lion found him, and it looked so ugly that its foe turned up his nose in disgust. Its legs were quite as long as the tiger had said, and its body covered with coarse black hair. It had a great mouth, with a row of sharp teeth a foot long; but its head was joined to the pudgy body by a neck as slender as a wasp's waist. This gave the Lion a hint of the best way to attack the creature, and as he knew it was easier to fight it asleep than awake, he gave a great spring and landed directly upon the monster's back. Then, with one blow of his heavy paw, all armed with sharp claws, he knocked the spider's head from its body. Jumping down, he watched it until the long legs stopped wiggling, when he knew it was quite dead.

The Lion went back to the opening where the beasts of the forest were waiting for him and said proudly:

"You need fear your enemy no longer."

Then the beasts bowed down to the Lion as their King, and he promised to come back and rule over them as soon as Dorothy was safely on her way to Kansas.

• ANALYZING THE SCENE •

STORY EVENT

A Story Event is an active change of a universal human value for one or more characters as a result of conflict (one character's desires clash with another's, or an environmental shift changes the universal human value).

A Working Scene contains at least one Story Event. To determine a scene's Story Event, answer these four Socratic questions:

1. The Action Story Component: What are the characters literally doing—that is, what are their micro on-the-surface actions?

The group enters a forest that only the Lion finds appealing and spends the night. In the morning the Lion confers with the animals in the forest and sets out to slay their enemy, which he does and assumes control of the territory.

2. The Worldview Story Component: What is the essential tactic of the characters—that is, what above-the-surface macro behaviors are they employing that are linked to a universal human value?

The Lion seizes opportunity courageously.

3. The Heroic Journey 2.0 Component: What beyond-the-surface universal human values have changed for one or more characters in the scene? Which one of those value changes is most important and should be included in the Story Grid Spreadsheet?

When in doubt, the Story Grid rule of thumb is to highlight the value that best aligns with the progress of the global human value at stake in the story. *The Wonderful Wizard of Oz* is an Action Story, which has a global value at stake of Life/Death. Throughout the Story Grid Spreadsheet, we'll track the ways life is threatened or enhanced scene by scene.

The value shift is clear for Dorothy and her companions, *Threatened to Safe*.

4. The Scene Event Synthesis: What Story Event sums up the scene's on-the-surface actions, essential above-the-surface worldview behavioral tactics, and beyond-the-surface value change? We will enter that event in the Story Grid Spreadsheet.

On their way to see Glinda the Good Witch, the Lion seizes opportunity by killing a great spider and ascends to king of the forest.

HOW THE SCENE ABIDES BY THE FIVE COMMANDMENTS OF STORYTELLING

Inciting Incident: Dorothy and the crew reach a dark beast-ridden forest.

Turning Point Progressive Complication: The beasts are terrorized by a giant spider and they want the Lion to kill it for them.

Crisis: Best bad choice. If the team does not get through the forest, they will not meet Glinda. If the Lion gets killed fighting the spider, the beasts will kill his friends.

Climax: The Lion kills the spider.

Resolution: The Lion is now king of the forest.

22

THE COUNTRY OF THE QUADLINGS

SCENE 22

The four travelers passed through the rest of the forest in safety, and when they came out from its gloom saw before them a steep hill, covered from top to bottom with great pieces of rock.

"That will be a hard climb," said **the Scarecrow**, "but we must get over the hill, nevertheless."

So he led the way and the others followed. They had nearly reached the first rock when they heard **a rough voice** cry out, "Keep back!"

"Who are you?" asked the Scarecrow.

Then a head showed itself over the rock and the same voice said, "This hill belongs to us, and we don't allow anyone to cross it."

"But we must cross it," said the Scarecrow. "We're going to the country of **the Quadlings**."

"But you shall not!" replied the voice, and there stepped from behind the rock the strangest man the travelers had ever seen.

He was quite short and stout and had a big head, which was flat at the top and supported by a thick neck full of wrinkles. But he had no arms at all, and, seeing this, the Scarecrow did not fear that so helpless a creature could prevent them from climbing the hill. So he said, "I'm

167

sorry not to do as you wish, but we must pass over your hill whether you like it or not," and he walked boldly forward.

As quick as lightning the man's head shot forward and his neck stretched out until the top of the head, where it was flat, struck the Scarecrow in the middle and sent him tumbling, over and over, down the hill. Almost as quickly as it came the head went back to the body, and the man laughed harshly as he said, "It isn't as easy as you think!"

A chorus of boisterous laughter came from the other rocks, and **Dorothy** saw hundreds of the armless Hammer-Heads upon the hillside, one behind every rock.

The Lion became quite angry at the laughter caused by the Scarecrow's mishap, and giving a loud roar that echoed like thunder, he dashed up the hill.

Again a head shot swiftly out, and the great Lion went rolling down the hill as if he had been struck by a cannon ball.

Dorothy ran down and helped the Scarecrow to his feet, and the Lion came up to her, feeling rather bruised and sore, and said, "It is useless to fight people with shooting heads; no one can withstand them."

"What can we do, then?" she asked.

"Call **the Winged Monkeys**," suggested the **Tin Woodman**. "You have still the right to command them once more."

"Very well," she answered, and putting on the Golden Cap she uttered the magic words. The Monkeys were as prompt as ever, and in a few moments the entire band stood before her.

"What are your commands?" inquired the **King of the Monkeys**, bowing low.

"Carry us over the hill to the country of the Quadlings," answered the girl.

"It shall be done," said the King, and at once the Winged Monkeys caught the four travelers and **Toto** up in their arms and flew away with them. As they passed over the hill the Hammer-Heads yelled with vexation, and shot their heads high in the air, but they could not reach the Winged Monkeys, which carried Dorothy and her comrades safely over the hill and set them down in the beautiful country of the Quadlings.

"This is the last time you can summon us," said the leader to Dorothy; "so good-bye and good luck to you."

"Good-bye, and thank you very much," returned the girl; and the Monkeys rose into the air and were out of sight in a twinkling.

The country of the Quadlings seemed rich and happy. There was field upon field of ripening grain, with well-paved roads running between, and pretty rippling brooks with strong bridges across them. The fences and houses and bridges were all painted bright red, just as they had been painted yellow in the country of **the Winkies** and blue in the country of **the Munchkins**. The Quadlings themselves, who were short and fat and looked chubby and good-natured, were dressed all in red, which showed bright against the green grass and the yellowing grain.

The Monkeys had set them down near a farmhouse, and the four travelers walked up to it and knocked at the door. It was opened by **the farmer's wife**, and when Dorothy asked for something to eat the woman gave them all a good dinner, with three kinds of cake and four kinds of cookies, and a bowl of milk for Toto.

"How far is it to the Castle of **Glinda**?" asked the child.

"It is not a great way," answered the farmer's wife. "Take the road to the South and you will soon reach it."

Thanking the good woman, they started afresh and walked by the fields and across the pretty bridges until they saw before them a very beautiful Castle. Before the gates were **three young girls**, dressed in handsome red uniforms trimmed with gold braid; and as Dorothy approached, one of them said to her:

"Why have you come to the South Country?"

"To see the Good Witch who rules here," she answered. "Will you take me to her?"

"Let me have your name, and I will ask Glinda if she will receive you." They told who they were, and the girl soldier went into the Castle. After a few moments she came back to say that Dorothy and the others were to be admitted at once.

STORY EVENT

A Story Event is an active change of a universal human value for one or more characters as a result of conflict (one character's desires clash with another's, or an environmental shift changes the universal human value).

A Working Scene contains at least one Story Event. To determine a scene's Story Event, answer these four Socratic questions:

1. The Action Story Component: What are the characters literally doing—that is, what are their micro on-the-surface actions?

The group contends with the armless beings guarding a rock face and blocking them from passage into Glinda's territory. They call the Winged Monkeys and eventually reach their destination.

2. The Worldview Story Component: What is the essential tactic of the characters—that is, what above-the-surface macro behaviors are they employing that are linked to a universal human value?

The group is a formidable problem-solving force overcoming obstacles that drop into their lives with unexpected force.

3. The Heroic Journey 2.0 Component: What beyond-the-surface universal human values have changed for one or more characters in the scene? Which one of those value changes is most important and should be included in the Story Grid Spreadsheet?

When in doubt, the Story Grid rule of thumb is to highlight the value that best aligns with the progress of the global human value at stake in the story. *The Wonderful Wizard of Oz* is an Action Story, which has a global value at stake of Life/Death. Throughout the Story Grid Spreadsheet, we'll track the ways life is threatened or enhanced scene by scene.

The value shift for Dorothy and her companions is clear, *Stymied to Successful.*

4. The Scene Event Synthesis: What Story Event sums up the scene's on-the-surface actions, essential above-the-surface worldview behavioral tactics, and beyond-the-surface value change? We will enter that event in the Story Grid Spreadsheet.

The Winged Monkeys fly the group over the Hammer-Head Rock pile and into Glinda the Good Witch's domain.

HOW THE SCENE ABIDES BY THE FIVE COMMANDMENTS OF STORYTELLING

Inciting Incident: The group comes to a tall rock wall guarded by Hammer-Heads.

Turning Point Progressive Complication: The Hammer-Heads cannot be beaten on the hill.

Crisis: Best bad choice. If the crew doesn't outmaneuver the Hammer-Heads, Dorothy will never make it to Kansas, but to fight them will prove fruitless.

Climax: Dorothy calls in her last wish from the winged monkeys.

Resolution: The crew makes it over the rock hill and to the land of Glinda the Good witch.

23

GLINDA THE GOOD WITCH GRANTS DOROTHY'S WISH

SCENE 23

Before they went to see **Glinda**, however, they were taken to a room of the Castle, where **Dorothy** washed her face and combed her hair, and **the Lion** shook the dust out of his mane, and **the Scarecrow** patted himself into his best shape, and **the Woodman** polished his tin and oiled his joints.

When they were all quite presentable they followed **the soldier girl** into a big room where **the Witch Glinda** sat upon a throne of rubies.

She was both beautiful and young to their eyes. Her hair was a rich red in color and fell in flowing ringlets over her shoulders. Her dress was pure white but her eyes were blue, and they looked kindly upon the little girl.

"What can I do for you, my child?" she asked.

Dorothy told the Witch all her story: how the cyclone had brought her to the Land of Oz, how she had found her companions, and of the wonderful adventures they had met with.

"My greatest wish now," she added, "is to get back to Kansas, for **Aunt Em** will surely think something dreadful has happened to me, and that will make her put on mourning; and unless the crops are better this year than they were last, I am sure **Uncle Henry** cannot afford it."

Glinda leaned forward and kissed the sweet, upturned face of the loving little girl.

"Bless your dear heart," she said, "I am sure I can tell you of a way to get back to Kansas." Then she added, "But, if I do, you must give me the Golden Cap."

"Willingly!" exclaimed Dorothy; "indeed, it is of no use to me now, and when you have it you can command the Winged Monkeys three times."

"And I think I shall need their service just those three times," answered Glinda, smiling.

Dorothy then gave her the Golden Cap, and the Witch said to the Scarecrow, "What will you do when Dorothy has left us?"

"I will return to the Emerald City," he replied, "for **Oz** has made me its ruler and the people like me. The only thing that worries me is how to cross the hill of the **Hammer-Heads.**"

"By means of the Golden Cap I shall command **the Winged Monkeys** to carry you to the gates of the Emerald City," said Glinda, "for it would be a shame to deprive **the people** of so wonderful a ruler."

"Am I really wonderful?" asked the Scarecrow.

"You are unusual," replied Glinda.

Turning to the **Tin Woodman**, she asked, "What will become of you when Dorothy leaves this country?"

He leaned on his axe and thought a moment. Then he said, "**The Winkies** were very kind to me, and wanted me to rule over them after **the Wicked Witch** died. I am fond of the Winkies, and if I could get back again to the Country of the West, I should like nothing better than to rule over them forever."

"My second command to the Winged Monkeys," said Glinda "will be that they carry you safely to the land of the Winkies. Your brain may not be so large to look at as those of the Scarecrow, but you are really brighter than he is—when you are well polished—and I am sure you will rule the Winkies wisely and well."

Then the Witch looked at the big, shaggy Lion and asked, "When Dorothy has returned to her own home, what will become of you?"

"Over the hill of the Hammer-Heads," he answered, "lies a grand old forest, and all **the beasts** that live there have made me their King. If I could only get back to this forest, I would pass my life very happily there."

"My third command to the Winged Monkeys," said Glinda, "shall be to carry you to your forest. Then, having used up the powers of the Golden Cap, I shall give it to the **King of the Monkeys**, that he and his band may thereafter be free for evermore."

The Scarecrow and the Tin Woodman and the Lion now thanked the Good Witch earnestly for her kindness; and Dorothy exclaimed:

"You are certainly as good as you are beautiful! But you have not yet told me how to get back to Kansas."

"Your Silver Shoes will carry you over the desert," replied Glinda. "If you had known their power you could have gone back to your Aunt Em the very first day you came to this country."

"But then I should not have had my wonderful brains!" cried the Scarecrow. "I might have passed my whole life in the farmer's cornfield."

"And I should not have had my lovely heart," said the Tin Woodman. "I might have stood and rusted in the forest till the end of the world."

"And I should have lived a coward forever," declared the Lion, "and no beast in all the forest would have had a good word to say to me."

"This is all true," said Dorothy, "and I am glad I was of use to these good friends. But now that each of them has had what he most desired, and each is happy in having a kingdom to rule besides, I think I should like to go back to Kansas."

"The Silver Shoes," said the Good Witch, "have wonderful powers. And one of the most curious things about them is that they can carry you to any place in the world in three steps, and each step will be made in the wink of an eye. All you have to do is to knock the heels together three times and command the shoes to carry you wherever you wish to go."

"If that is so," said the child joyfully, "I will ask them to carry me back to Kansas at once."

She threw her arms around the Lion's neck and kissed him, patting his big head tenderly. Then she kissed the Tin Woodman, who was weeping in a way most dangerous to his joints. But she hugged the soft, stuffed body of the Scarecrow in her arms instead of kissing his painted face, and found she was crying herself at this sorrowful parting from her loving comrades.

Glinda the Good stepped down from her ruby throne to give the little girl a good-bye kiss, and Dorothy thanked her for all the kindness she had shown to her friends and herself.

Dorothy now took Toto up solemnly in her arms, and having said one last good-bye she clapped the heels of her shoes together three times, saying:

"Take me home to Aunt Em!"

Instantly she was whirling through the air, so swiftly that all she could see or feel was the wind whistling past her ears.

The Silver Shoes took but three steps, and then she stopped so suddenly that she rolled over upon the grass several times before she knew where she was.

At length, however, she sat up and looked about her.

"Good gracious!" she cried.

For she was sitting on the broad Kansas prairie, and just before her was the new farmhouse Uncle Henry built after the cyclone had carried away the old one. **Uncle Henry** was milking the cows in the barnyard, and Toto had jumped out of her arms and was running toward the barn, barking furiously.

Dorothy stood up and found she was in her stocking-feet. For the Silver Shoes had fallen off in her flight through the air, and were lost forever in the desert.

• ANALYZING THE SCENE •

STORY EVENT

A Story Event is an active change of a universal human value for one or more characters as a result of conflict (one character's desires clash with another's, or an environmental shift changes the universal human value).

A Working Scene contains at least one Story Event. To determine a scene's Story Event, answer these four Socratic questions:

1. The Action Story Component: What are the characters literally doing—that is, what are their micro on-the-surface actions?

The group meets with Glinda the Good Witch from the South, and she settles their troubles.

2. The Worldview Story Component: What is the essential tactic of the characters—that is, what above-the-surface macro behaviors are they employing that are linked to a universal human value?

The group puts their trust in the wisdom of a benevolent authority figure.

3. The Heroic Journey 2.0 Component: What beyond-the-surface universal human values have changed for one or more characters in the scene? Which one of those value changes is most important and should be included in the Story Grid Spreadsheet?

When in doubt, the Story Grid rule of thumb is to highlight the value that best aligns with the progress of the global human value at stake in the story. *The Wonderful Wizard of Oz* is an Action Story, which has a global value at stake of Life/Death. Throughout the Story Grid Spreadsheet, we'll track the ways life is threatened or enhanced scene by scene.

The value shift for Dorothy is clear, *Uncertainty to Stability*. And *Unknown to Known*.

4. The Scene Event Synthesis: What Story Event sums up the scene's on-the-surface actions, essential above-the-surface worldview behavioral tactics, and beyond-the-surface value change? We will enter that event in the Story Grid Spreadsheet.

Dorothy trades the Golden Cap to get back to Kansas, and Glinda uses the wishes locked within to send the Lion, the Scarecrow, and the Tin Woodman home. Glinda tells Dorothy to command her silver shoes to take her back to Kansas.

HOW THE SCENE ABIDES BY THE FIVE COMMANDMENTS OF STORYTELLING

Inciting Incident: The team enters Glinda's throne room.

Turning Point Progressive Complication: Glinda won't tell Dorothy how to get home without her handing over the Golden Cap.

Crisis: Irreconcilable Goods: If Glinda grants Dorothy's wish, her friends will be stranded. If she doesn't, Dorothy will be stranded.

Climax: Dorothy willingly gives Glinda the Golden Cap.

Resolution: All four find home.

24

HOME AGAIN

SCENE 24

Aunt Em had just come out of the house to water the cabbages when she looked up and saw **Dorothy** running toward her.

"My darling child!" she cried, folding the little girl in her arms and covering her face with kisses. "Where in the world did you come from?"

"From the Land of **Oz**," said Dorothy gravely. "And here is **Toto**, too. And oh, Aunt Em! I'm so glad to be at home again!"

• ANALYZING THE SCENE •

STORY EVENT

A Story Event is an active change of a universal human value for one or more characters as a result of conflict (one character's desires clash with another's, or an environmental shift changes the universal human value).

A Working Scene contains at least one Story Event. To determine a scene's Story Event, answer these four Socratic questions:

1. The Action Story Component: What are the characters literally doing—that is, what are their micro on-the-surface actions?

Aunt Em is watering cabbages. Dorothy runs toward her.

2. The Worldview Story Component: What is the essential tactic of the characters—that is, what above-the-surface macro behaviors are they employing that are linked to a universal human value?

Dorothy gratefully attunes to her everyday reality.

3. The Heroic Journey 2.0 Component: What beyond-the-surface universal human values have changed for one or more characters in the scene? Which one of those value changes is most important and should be included in the Story Grid Spreadsheet?

Dorothy returns safely home to her family in Kansas.

When in doubt, the Story Grid rule of thumb is to highlight the value that best aligns with the progress of the global human value at stake in the story. *The Wonderful Wizard of Oz* is an Action Story, which has a global value at stake of Life/Death. Throughout the Story Grid Spreadsheet, we'll track the ways life is threatened or enhanced scene by scene.

The value shift is clear, *Exiled to Home*.

4. **The Scene Event Synthesis:** What Story Event sums up the scene's on-the-surface actions, essential above-the-surface worldview behavioral tactics, and beyond-the-surface value change? We will enter that event in the Story Grid Spreadsheet.

Dorothy arrives home and rushes into Aunt Em's arms.

HOW THE SCENE ABIDES BY THE FIVE COMMANDMENTS OF STORYTELLING

Inciting Incident: Dorothy runs toward Aunt Em.

Turning Point Progressive Complication: Aunt Em is taken aback because she's been gone so long.

Crisis: Best bad choice. If Dorothy tells the truth about where's she's been, Aunt Em may think she's lost her mind. If she doesn't tell the truth, she'll never be able to live authentically.

Climax: Dorothy tells Aunt Em that she was in the land of Oz.

Resolution: Open ending, but Dorothy is home again.

ABOUT THE AUTHOR

SHAWN COYNE created, developed, and expanded the story analysis and problem-solving methodology The Story Grid throughout his quarter-century-plus book publishing career. A seasoned story editor, book publisher and ghostwriter, Coyne has also co-authored *The Ones Who Hit the Hardest: The Steelers, The Cowboys, the '70s and the Fight for America's Soul* with Chad Millman and *Cognitive Dominance: A Brain Surgeon's Quest to Out-Think Fear* with Mark McLaughlin, M.D. With his friend and editorial client Steven Pressfield, Coyne runs Black Irish Entertainment LLC, publisher of the cult classic book *The War of Art*. With his friend and editorial client Tim Grahl, Coyne oversees the Story Grid Universe, LLC, which includes Story Grid University and Story Grid Publishing.

ABOUT THE EDITOR

LESLIE WATTS is a Story Grid Certified Editor, writer, and podcaster based in Austin, Texas. She's been writing for as long as she can remember—from her sixth-grade magazine about cats to writing practice while drafting opinions for an appellate court judge. As an editor, Leslie helps fiction and nonfiction clients write epic stories that matter. She believes writers become better storytellers through study and practice and that editors owe a duty of care to help writers with specific and supportive guidance. You can find her online at Writership.com.

NOTES

THE HJ2.0 GLOBAL INCITING INCIDENT

1. Daniel Simons and Christopher Chabris, "Selective Attention Test," YouTube video, 1:21, posted by Daniel Simons, March 10, 2010, https://www.youtube.com/watch?v=vJG698U2Mvo).

Made in the USA
Las Vegas, NV
18 September 2021

30567591R00138